FRANK LLOYD WRIGHT

Constantin Brancu
The essence

FRANK
LLOYD
WRIGHT

Quercus

CONTENTS

THE LIFE OF FRANK LLOYD WRIGHT

FRANK LLOYD WRIGHT, who has strong claims to be considered North America's greatest architect, lived from 1867 to 1959. His life therefore began in the steam age and ended in the space age. When he was born, American architecture was drawing on a range of styles, some based on the architecture of medieval Europe, some on more recent examples from France. By the time he died, a new, distinctive kind of architecture had evolved, responsive to the needs of people living both in the cities and in the open spaces of the USA. Frank Lloyd Wright was one of the most important creators of this new architecture, as well as the designer of some of North America's most beautiful and memorable buildings.

Frank Lloyd Wright was born in 1867 in the town of Richland Center, Wisconsin. His parents were William Carey Wright, a preacher and musician, and Anna Lloyd Jones Wright, a schoolteacher who was 14 years younger than her husband. William Wright had various short-term jobs preaching and giving music lessons, but found it hard to find permanent employment, so when Frank was young the family moved several times as William looked for work. His mother was a more rooted personality. She came from a family of Welsh religious dissenters who had arrived in the USA in 1844. Independent-minded, strongly religious and immersed in the culture of Transcendentalism that was so strong in the USA in the 19th century, Anna was to have the more enduring influence on her son.

An architect's education
When he was a boy, Wright was educated by his mother, who started a small school run on the principles established by the German educationalist Friedrich Froebel. The Froebel system stressed learning from nature and fostered spatial awareness. This educational system promoted analytical thinking by encouraging children to take objects apart and reassemble them, and emphasized the patterns and geometries that lay behind the things that made up the physical world. In addition, Froebel stressed the spiritual side of life – helping to show that the spiritual and material spheres were actually aspects of the same world. With its emphasis on design, spatial awareness and analysis, a Froebel education was a good one for an architect.

In the early 1880s, William and Anna's marriage began to fall apart and in 1884 the couple divorced. Frank, their eldest child and only son, had to go to work to help support his mother and sisters. He joined the office of the engineer Allan Conover in Madison, Wisconsin, where he worked while also studying engineering at the University of Wisconsin. This engineering background stood Wright in good stead when he came to design his own buildings – it was a very American and pragmatic training for an architect, and it helped him when he wanted to push structures in new and challenging directions. Wright's time with Conover was a useful apprenticeship.

Working with Sullivan
But Madison offered limited opportunities for an aspiring architect, so at the age of 20, Wright left for Chicago. Here he worked first in the office of the architect J. Lyman Silsbee and then, after a year, for the prominent Chicago firm of Adler and Sullivan.

Architect Louis Sullivan quickly recognized Wright's abilities, and the young architect was soon a key figure in the office of Adler and Sullivan, who were designing landmark buildings in Chicago and other cities. Working with Sullivan on major structures such as the Wainwright, Schiller and Auditorium

Buildings gave Wright experience at the cutting edge of architecture. It also gave him contacts. Soon he was moonlighting – doing designs for his own clients in the evenings while designing in Sullivan's office by day. Wright was later to claim that Sullivan fired him because he took on these unofficial commissions, although there is some doubt about this story.

The year 1893 proved to be a turning point for Wright. At the Chicago International Exposition that year he saw his first Japanese building, the Japanese National Pavilion. With its wooden beams, overhanging roofs and fluid internal spaces, it was to have a huge influence on Wright's architecture. The other pivotal event that year came when Daniel Burnham, probably America's most successful architect at the time, offered to pay for Wright to study classical architecture in Paris and Rome for six years, followed by a guarantee of a job in Burnham's office. It was a dream offer, but Wright turned Burnham down. He didn't want to study the ancient, European conventions of classical architecture. The young architect stayed in the Midwest to open his own office and pursue a more modern, more American dream.

Making it new

'Make it new,' said the poet Ezra Pound, pointing the way forward for the American artist in the 20th century. The buildings that Wright designed in the years around the turn of the century saw him developing his own style and creating a new, essentially American, kind of architecture – inventive, problem-solving and responsive both to clients' needs and to the American landscape. This was the period in which Wright designed the Larkin Company Administration Building in Buffalo, New York, a groundbreaking office building that provided comfortable working conditions for some 1,800 workers and pioneered the use of new technologies such as air conditioning. Equally revolutionary was Unity Temple, Oak Park, Illinois, the first church in America to be built of exposed concrete, a material that Wright had quickly learned to handle beautifully.

Meanwhile, a string of houses in the years leading up to the First World War saw Wright developing looser plans in which one living space flowed into the next, in which rooms with generous windows were sheltered by equally lavish overhanging eaves, and in which designs were worked out with the individual client's requirements clearly in mind. Out of this group of designs, Wright developed what he called the Prairie House. These low-slung, ground-hugging houses often had cross-shaped footprints, spread out in all directions to take advantage of the sun's position at different times of day. With their horizontal profiles, roomy interiors and the way they are grounded in the landscape, they redefined the American house.

The Prairie Houses were built for rich clients, people with live-in servants and the money to build on a big scale; but Wright also wanted to produce a more 'democratic' architecture. He began to design smaller houses such as the 'Fireproof House for $5,000', which he published in the *Ladies' Home Journal* in 1906. He would return to such ideas later in his career, looking for new ways to build houses on a tight budget.

Crisis

In 1909, as he came to the end of his sequence of Prairie Houses, a crisis occurred in Wright's life. He began an affair with Mamah Borthwick Cheney, the wife of a client, and left his wife Catherine and their six children to visit Europe with Mamah. When Wright returned to the USA he learned that Catherine would not grant him a divorce, and he set up home with Mamah in a new house, Taliesin, which he built in Spring Green, Wisconsin. But in 1914 disaster struck: Julian Carlton, a servant who had been threatened with dismissal, ran amok, set the house on fire and killed several people, including Mamah.

The following years were difficult ones for Wright. He spent much of the period between 1914 and 1923 in Japan designing Tokyo's Imperial Hotel, returning to North America from time to time to work on the few other jobs he had – most notably Hollyhock House, the outstanding home that he built in Los Angeles for oil heiress Aline Barnsdall. The Tokyo hotel was a notable success, especially when Wright's tremor-resistant construction method was proved to work during the disastrous earthquake of 1923. But it kept the architect away from the USA for long periods, and his work in North America declined. However, during his absence in Japan his son Lloyd, also an architect, had found clients in California; in addition, Wright and Catherine had finally divorced in 1922 and he had married the sculptor Miriam Noel. He decided to open an office in Los Angeles.

California seemed to offer a new beginning. Wright developed a way of designing houses constructed of cast concrete blocks, and four of these were built. But Wright's capacity for spending money was far greater than his income warranted and his emotional life was still in turmoil – Miriam turned out to be addicted to morphine, and on one occasion threatened Wright with a knife. Scarcely a year after his marriage to Miriam, Wright found consolation with another woman: he met and fell in love with Olgivanna Hinzenberg, a Montenegro-born dancer and wife of the Russian architect Valdemar Hinzenberg. But the architect's troubles were far from over. By 1926 he was deeply in debt and his bank took possession of Taliesin. Meanwhile, the jealous Miriam pursued Wright, Olgivanna and their baby, threatening to have Wright arrested for a violation of the Mann Act, a law that targeted traffickers of immigrant prostitutes.

ABOVE Frank Lloyd Wright instructs a bulldozer driver at Spring Green, Wisconsin, in 1945. The ground is being prepared for improvements to the architect's property – probably the construction of dams to create a small lake to regulate water flow through the adjacent farmland.

In 1927 Wright was granted a divorce from Miriam; the following year he married Olgivanna, and the pair tried to sort out their lives. But as the Great Depression struck, architectural work was still harder to come by. With Olgivanna's encouragement, Wright turned to writing and lecturing as a way of both earning a living and publicizing his work and ideas. He published many articles, an *Autobiography* and a book about urban planning, *The Disappearing City*. In addition, he turned Taliesin into a combination of communal settlement, architecture school and architectural practice by inviting people to pay him to serve as his apprentices.

Olgivanna remained central to the life of the Taliesin Fellowship as a self-appointed spiritual leader, adviser and manager second only to Wright himself in importance and influence. She helped to maintain the strictly hierarchical system of the Fellowship (indeed 'Fellowship' was an inappropriate name), in which everyone had to defer to Wright and Olgivanna. The architect was always referred to as 'Mr Wright', and criticism of his ideas was frowned upon.

New directions

The 1930s saw Wright return to his ideas about a more democratic architecture. He began a series of houses for middle-income Americans that were more compact and cheaper to build than his earlier, lavish Prairie Houses. These houses, which Wright called 'Usonian Houses', were usually built on one level and based on a modular design, often using standard components and lots of timber in the structure. They were houses for a modern lifestyle, for people without servants.

The Usonian Houses had an open plan, with the kitchen often placed centrally so that the woman of the house could keep an eye on her children while preparing meals. They lacked the large stable blocks or garages of the Prairie Houses – if the family had an automobile, it could be kept in a carport formed from an overhanging flat roof. The accommodation was designed for people who lived in the machine age, with labour-saving domestic appliances. But they were also meant to keep people in touch with the land, their L-shaped or tadpole-shaped plans opening on to gardens through numerous glazed doors.

Wright designed many variations on the Usonian theme, and this work kept his practice busy in the 1930s, in addition spreading his ideas through a new stratum of American society. At the same time, he took on work for rich clients who admired his ideas of 'organic architecture'. These major houses included Fallingwater (for store owner Edgar J. Kaufmann) and Wingspread (for Herbert Johnson, of the Johnson Wax Company, for whom Wright also designed a notable headquarters building).

The architect continued his writing and proselytizing too. Some of his boldest ideas were embodied in projects that, although they were never built, demonstrated what Wright saw as the way forward for American architecture and urban planning. The greatest example was a project called Broadacre City, an 'ideal' city design that Wright developed and revised at various times during his working life. The key idea behind this concept was that each American family should have one acre (0.4 ha) of land on which to build their house.

The successes of the 1930s and 1940s brought Wright wider recognition, although other architects were slow to follow up his ideas. However, in 1949 Wright was finally presented with the Gold Medal of the American Institute of Architects, showing that his innovative work was at last recognized by his country's architectural establishment.

The late work

Wright continued to design through his eighties, and in the 1950s created several of his most memorable buildings, both large and small. He developed the concept of the Usonian House still further, creating what he called the 'Usonian Automatic', a concrete-block house so easy to build that, in theory at least, much of the construction work could be done by the clients themselves. Wright's last years also saw the designs for major buildings such as New York's Guggenheim Museum and the Beth Sholom Synagogue in Philadelphia. Although some of the late buildings – such as the buildings for Marin County in California – have been seen by some as marking a decline in his powers, structures such as the Guggenheim Museum show that, right up to the end of his life, Wright was capable of highly original designs that explored new architectural directions.

Frank Lloyd Wright died on 9 April 1959, in Phoenix, Arizona. The commitment of his associates and apprentices in the Taliesin Fellowship meant that a number of major projects, including the Guggenheim Museum, still under construction at the time of his death were brought to completion. Among his 500 built structures, some 400 still survive as clear and lasting evidence of the multifaceted genius of America's greatest architect.

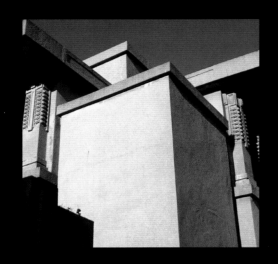

FRANK LLOYD WRIGHT OFTEN FOUND himself going out on a limb, an experience he clearly enjoyed. As a young man he showed no desire to follow the way of life of either his father (a preacher) or his mother's male relatives (who were mostly farmers). He wanted to be an architect, but when he began work in the profession, he found there, too, he was going his own way. As a young architect in the office of Adler and Sullivan, a great practice at the height of their success, he was drawn not to their large public building projects, but to the residential work that did not interest the senior partners. But even here he showed signs that he wanted to design houses that were different from the norm, buildings less reliant on European traditions than those produced by other American architects.

The buildings in this chapter show Wright finding his way as an architect after he left the office of Adler and Sullivan and began to establish his own methods. They see him thinking projects through from the very basics, so that he could create, for example, a radical design for a church (Unity Temple) and a new kind of wind pump (the Romeo and Juliet Windmill). They show how he enthusiastically embraced new materials, as with the poured concrete of Unity Temple. They find him looking in unusual directions for work and inspiration, especially to Japan, for Tokyo's Imperial Hotel. And, most remarkably, they see him embracing new technologies in the air-conditioned, double-glazed Larkin Building.

As his career developed, Wright fused all these elements in an architecture that was unlike anything else, a way of building that was painstakingly thought through rather than being a slavish copy of previous architects or styles. For the first time, Wright claimed, the USA had its own, thoroughly American, kind of architecture.

ROOTS OF AN ARCHITECT

Frank Lloyd Wright House

In 1889 the 21-year-old Frank Lloyd Wright fell in love with Catherine Tobin, whom he had met at a social gathering at his church in Oak Park, Chicago. Naturally, when the couple planned to get married, the young architect wanted to build a home for himself and his wife. The building he designed, a compact house dominated by a large, dramatic gable, stands out from its neighbours; but, clad in shingles, the house also uses traditional materials. Like so many of his later buildings, this first house is an enthralling mixture of old and new.

Location
Oak Park, Illinois

Client
The architect

Date
1889

Main materials
Wood, shingle, brick

Wright and Catherine were eager to marry, but the young architect had no job security and no money. He told his boss, Louis Sullivan, about his plans, and Sullivan immediately called in his partner, Dankmar Adler. 'What do you say to a five-year contract?' asked Sullivan. Adler was agreeable and Wright got his security. Emboldened by Sullivan's support, Wright then asked his boss for a loan to build a house for Catherine and himself. Sullivan agreed, advancing Wright $5,000 to buy some land and build a modest house in Oak Park.

Old and new So a year after he began working for Adler and Sullivan, Wright designed his marital home. The new house was Wright's first independent building, and, like so many of his later houses, is a rich mixture of the old and the new. It is a shingle-clad building, the exterior dominated by a huge gable – a bold architectural statement that immediately impresses and makes the building stand out. Shingles were a popular and traditional wall-cladding – there were 'shingle-style' houses all over the USA, especially in the east. But Wright did something quite dramatic and striking with the style. The big sweeping gable and the bold strips of casement windows beneath it owe a lot to the designs of the great British Arts and Crafts architect C.F.A. Voysey, and perhaps something to the Scottish master Charles Rennie Mackintosh. No doubt Wright had been reading the architectural magazines.

RIGHT Leaded windowpanes became one of Wright's hallmarks. In this early house, they are used in a conventional diamond pattern, as they were in many other 19th-century buildings. The architect prized them for the multifaceted way they reflect the light, which is more 'alive' than with large panes of plate glass.

OPPOSITE From the outside, the most striking feature of the Frank Lloyd Wright house is the large gable that sweeps down to first-floor level, casting strong shadows. This gable, together with the building's wings and bays, shows how the young architect was already developing his skill with the handling of shapes and forms.

Frank Lloyd Wright House
14

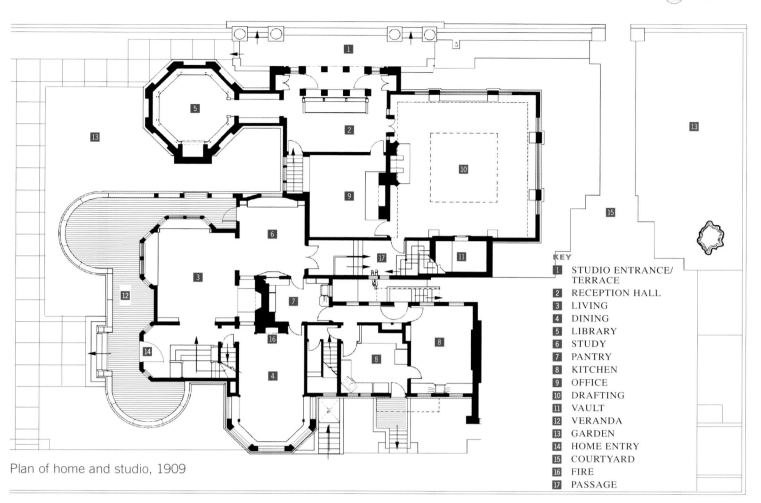

Plan of home and studio, 1909

KEY

1. STUDIO ENTRANCE/ TERRACE
2. RECEPTION HALL
3. LIVING
4. DINING
5. LIBRARY
6. STUDY
7. PANTRY
8. KITCHEN
9. OFFICE
10. DRAFTING
11. VAULT
12. VERANDA
13. GARDEN
14. HOME ENTRY
15. COURTYARD
16. FIRE
17. PASSAGE

ABOVE This plan shows the main floor of Wright's house and studio in Oak Park. The original house is to the bottom left – to its four rooms at the front Wright later added the kitchen complex with the children's playroom above it. The part of the building at the top of the plan, including the drafting room and octagonal library, was added when Wright extended the building in the late 1890s (see pages 26–29).

OPPOSITE Inside the house, Wright used the roof line to create distinctive ceilings, their form emphasized by a series of dark bands. Although this bedroom is not an especially large space, the high ceiling makes it feel larger, while the windows open towards the garden to create a still greater sense of space.

Arts and Crafts details
Inside, the hearth in its inglenook, the fire surrounded by a great sweeping semi-circular arch of brickwork, also has a hint of Voysey and the British Arts and Crafts movement. The hearth is the focus of the interior and, though the inglenook is small, it is very much at the heart of the house. The eye is led to it as you enter the main living room through the hall. Other details – strips of windows set quite high in the walls, built-in seating and wooden floors – also pay tribute to the Arts and Crafts movement. To 21st-century eyes, the effect of the house is old-fashioned, looking back to the Victorian era. But in the 1880s, the work of Voysey and his colleagues was new, and the North American shingle style was current. The house would have seemed up-to-date to contemporaries.

Design innovations
It is also the start of Wright's long architectural exploration of house design. As originally built, the house was quite small and compact. The first floor comprised just four rooms, the entrance hall, living room, kitchen and dining room usual in standard American 'four-square' houses of the time. But Wright was already developing these spaces in his own distinctive way – centring the plan on the fireplace, making the entrance and living space flow into each other, and creating a precise geometry for the staircase.

Wright also developed an effective way of organizing the interior, so that the many apparently random elements (windows, doorways, openings, lengths of wall, and so on) appeared neither too random nor disorganized. This is seen clearly in the living room, where Wright used a pale band at the top of the wall to bind the wall to the ceiling, allowing all the other elements to float beneath it, at once free and yet disciplined.

The architect's calling card
An architect's house plays many roles. As well as a living space for the designer and his family, it can also be a calling card to demonstrate what the architect can do, a workplace and a place for experimenting with new designs. While he was still working for Adler and Sullivan, Wright had no pressing need for a workspace at home – the studio extension to the house came later (see pages 26–29). But as Wright's family grew, he extended the house, trying out new design ideas that were later adapted in his other buildings.

Wright and Catherine eventually had six children, so one requirement was for a playroom. The architect responded in 1895 with a striking room – again wooden-floored and lit by strips of windows, but this time topped with an astonishing semi-circular vaulted ceiling. It is a big room, with a fireplace at one end, and became a favourite for family gatherings as well as a space for the children to play. Its rather grand vaulted space also shows Wright flexing his wings, demonstrating that, in addition to the friendly, domestic spaces of the main house, he could produce something more dramatic. He was soon to develop still more drama in the houses he designed for clients and in a range of other kinds of buildings that established him, in the 1890s and the early 1900s, as an architect of staggering originality.

Blossom House

With its pale-painted wooden clapboard, the Blossom House recalls the buildings of colonial North America. It is unlike anything else Frank Lloyd Wright built, and might look more at home in New England than in Chicago, but shows the architect able to look to the past for inspiration (and perhaps to respond to the wishes of a traditionally minded client), coming up in the process with a design that is fresh and pleasing to look at.

Location
Chicago, Illinois

Client
George Blossom

Date
1892

Main materials
Wood, clapboard siding

Wright's employers, Adler and Sullivan, were among the most successful American architects of their time. When Wright joined their firm they were rising stars in Chicago, and had just been commissioned to design the city's Auditorium Building, a large opera house which, it was hoped, would put the city firmly on the cultural map. Young Wright was set to work on the drawings for the Auditorium as soon as he joined the office of Adler and Sullivan, and he was involved with their other large-scale projects too.

The freelance architect
It was a good time to be working in the office of an up-and-coming firm in an expanding American city. But Wright was ambitious, and wanted to design buildings of his own. Luckily for Wright, Adler and Sullivan were not much interested in working on houses, so when a client came along looking for a house the young architect sometimes picked up the commission on a freelance basis. Thus he was able to do the first of his own house designs at weekends, while also having the security of working for a large firm during the week.

It's not certain how Wright's bosses reacted to their young architect's parallel career. Wright later claimed that when Sullivan found out about his freelance work, the older architect fired him. But Wright had a liking for dramatic stories about himself and Sullivan probably knew what was going on. His brother even lived on the same street as two of Wright's 'moonlighting' commissions. One of these was a house for insurance executive George Blossom on Kenwood Avenue.

This house shows that the young Wright could design in a classical idiom. The Blossom House has pilasters rising the full height of the outside walls, a large semi-circular porch supported by classical columns, and several three-section or 'Venetian' windows that come straight from the classical textbooks.

Spatial innovations
From the street, Blossom House looks symmetrical, ordered, and very traditional. But inside, it's not like this at all. The plan is close to being square, with the main living room arranged across the middle. However, this main room is placed off-centre, and the route from the entrance hall to the other main space, the dining room, entails crossing the living room diagonally, rather than tracing a direct, straight route as one would expect in a classical house. Other elements of the plan, such as a large semi-circular bay in the dining room, are also off-centre.

Another feature that makes the interior much less conventional than the exterior is the way the rooms connect with each other. They are less like rooms, more like interpenetrating spaces, because they are linked not by doors but by wide semicircular arches, so that the entrance hall merges into the living room, the living room into the dining room. The arches mark the boundaries between one room and the next but also open up the view into the next room, making the interior space fluid. This was a notion that Wright was to take much further in his later houses.

The Arts and Crafts influence
The interior has an Arts and Crafts atmosphere, not unlike Wright's own house. White walls and the curving strip of windows in the dining room, for example, set this tone. The windows here are casements (opening on hinges, like doors), not the vertical sash windows that were more common in North America at the time, There are patterns of leading in the glass, too, again alluding to the medieval inspiration of Arts and Crafts architects such as Voysey, and American masters such as Henry Hobson Richardson. The staircase, set off to the right of the living room and partly screened behind vertical wooden bars, is another detail that seems to come from this tradition. Such details in this poised classical house show how happily Wright could combine styles.

OPPOSITE The formal façades and pale siding make the Blossom House seem one of Wright's more conventional designs. But even here, the large rounded porch, protruding far into the garden, looks forward to the way the architect would use porches and balconies in his later, more radical work to bring house and surroundings together.

RIGHT In the interior of the house, the mix of pale walls, wooden panelling and beams – all well made and beautifully finished – shows Wright working confidently in an idiom influenced by the designers of the Arts and Crafts movement. The rounded arch, a key motif in this house, contrasts happily with the rectangular fireplace.

Winslow House
18

Winslow House

For many, the home Frank Lloyd Wright designed for manufacturer William H. Winslow was his first great house. The strong composition of its main façade, using the contrasting colours and decorative effects of brick, stone and plaster surmounted by a deeply overhanging roof, is beautifully assured. The interiors too are carefully finished, with the use of fine woodwork and restrained decoration, to make a setting perfect for a client with an active interest in the visual arts.

Location
River Forest, Illinois
Client
William Herman Winslow
Date
1894
Main materials
Brick, stone, exterior plaster

As a manufacturer of ornamental ironwork, William Winslow had often done business with the firm of Adler and Sullivan, and knew their work and their style well. He also knew very well that they were not designers of houses; so when he wanted a house for himself, rather than approach Louis Sullivan, Winslow went to Wright, who had just left the firm to set up on his own. It helped that Wright lived not far from the lot Winslow had bought for his house and that several of the architect's 'moonlighting' houses were in the neighbourhood.

An ideal client
Winslow was interesting in another way. In his spare time he ran the Auvergne Press, where he printed fine, hand-made books, including *The House Beautiful* by the Unitarian minister William C. Gannett. Wright designed the book and drew illustrations for it, identifying closely with Gannett's views, which saw the house as a kind of shrine of family love and culture. Winslow, then, was the ideal client for Wright – a man who wanted the best for himself and could publicize the architect's ideas about house building and design.

Wright produced a building worthy of his client. From a distance, the front of the Winslow House is a deceptively simple, bold composition. There is a brick first floor with windows and a door surrounded in white; a darker-coloured upper floor; and a hipped roof with a generous overhang, throwing the dark upper floor into shadow. In strong overhead sunlight, that dark band and dark shadow have the effect of making the roof seem to float above the brickwork, apparently hovering there supported only by the darkness.

Ornament, materials and design
Look closer, and the details reveal their subtleties. The masonry of the lower floor is made of 'Roman' brick – long, thin bricks that give a rich texture to the walls. The panel containing the central door and flanking windows is adorned with decorative tiles. The upper floor is covered with decorative plasterwork. This decoration gives the façade a feeling of richness, as if the good ornamental taste of architect and client reveal themselves to the full when you get close to the building. This interplay between ornament, materials and overall design is something that Wright learned from Sullivan. No doubt the manufacturer of decorative ironwork saw it as something to admire in both Wright and his master.

The other striking thing about the exterior is the strong horizontal emphasis. This was to become a major theme in Wright's houses. It fits with his ideas about architecture being organic, and about the way in which buildings should have an affinity with the ground. Many of Wright's later houses seem to hug the ground or emerge from the very earth. The Winslow House is not 'ground-hugging' in the way that later Wright buildings are. Formal and symmetrical, it is much less organic than the later houses. But it still has this marked horizontal quality.

LEFT Strict symmetry, a clear visual distinction between the floors, and the pale surround to the central doorway give the street front of the Winslow House a highly formal quality that is quite unusual in a Wright House. The careful and resourceful use of materials and colours, however – restrained in palette but rich in texture – is typical of the architect's work.

The interiors
The horizontal quality is achieved against the odds because the Winslow House is actually on three levels. As well as the two floors visible from the main façade, there is a third, hidden in the roof and lit only from a dormer at the rear. This third floor provided rooms for the Winslows' servants. Wright was later to resist putting servants' rooms in attics, bringing them down to lower levels into better-lit, more comfortable spaces that are seen by commentators as more 'democratic'. But in the Winslow House the servants are tucked away in the roof, so that their rooms do not interrupt the pure lines of the main front of the house.

The main interiors are lighter, and embody Wright's ideas about interrelated spaces and changing floor and ceiling levels. They feel much less formal than the classically symmetrical entrance front, but, fluid as they are, they incorporate traditional elements – arches, elegant ornament, rich materials, bow windows with fitted seating – in designs of great warmth.

The stable block
At the back of the Winslow House was the stable block. This too exhibited many Wright hallmarks, such as overhanging roofs and a horizontal emphasis. But the stable buildings were made all the more remarkable because Wright built them around an existing tree, which emerged dramatically from the stable roof to continue pushing out new shoots and branches above the tiles. Wright played this trick in several of his buildings. It was a device that delighted people looking at the building from the outside, but could frustrate owners because the gasket Wright devised to 'seal' the point where the roof covering met the tree trunk had a habit of leaking. But in the Winslow stable block, which was also home to the owner's printing press, this mattered rather less than in the residential part of the house, and it was another of Wright's ways of bringing building and nature together in unusual and memorable ways.

ABOVE This large semi-circular bay, its strip of windows ensuring that it is well lit at all times of the day, is one of the most inviting parts of the house. It is a surprise to come across this rounded space in a building that places such a strong emphasis on rectangles and symmetry.

OPPOSITE This view from the reception hall towards the library of the Winslow House shows the traditional style of the interior. Wooden panelling, with moulded architraves and door surrounds, is topped with delicate friezes and everything is bathed with soft light from the generous windows.

BELOW The octagonal columns and protruding oriel window on the stable block of the Winslow House show the architect's interest in unusual geometrical forms, and his confident handling of them. It is a surprise to come across shapes like these next to the otherwise resolutely four-square main house.

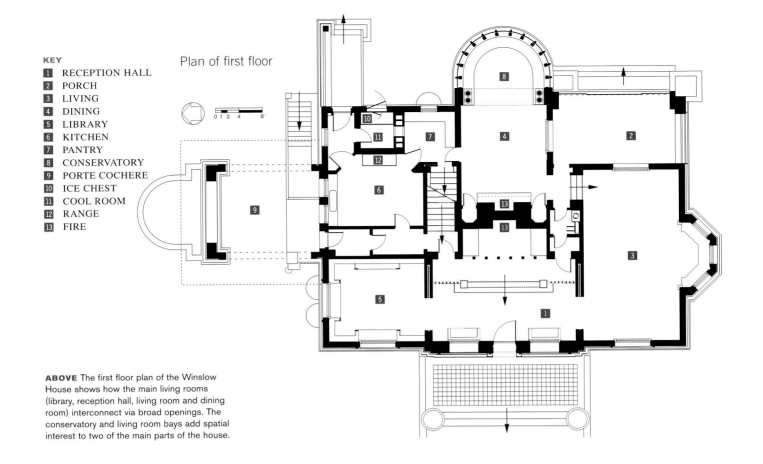

KEY

1. RECEPTION HALL
2. PORCH
3. LIVING
4. DINING
5. LIBRARY
6. KITCHEN
7. PANTRY
8. CONSERVATORY
9. PORTE COCHERE
10. ICE CHEST
11. COOL ROOM
12. RANGE
13. FIRE

Plan of first floor

ABOVE The first floor plan of the Winslow House shows how the main living rooms (library, reception hall, living room and dining room) interconnect via broad openings. The conservatory and living room bays add spatial interest to two of the main parts of the house.

Roloson Row Houses

This group of four row houses converted from earlier buildings shows Wright using a style of stonework that owes something to the early work of his mentor Louis Sullivan. The buildings have none of the Gothic ornament of many late 19th-century houses of this type, but their groups of large windows divided by uprights of stone are somewhat Tudor in appearance, while their grid-like layout seems almost to predict the aesthetics of modernism. Each façade sits under a steeply pitched gable, a remnant of the earlier building, which Wright originally wanted to remove.

Location
Chicago, Illinois

Client
Robert W. Roloson

Date
1894

Main material
Stone

After he had spent a year or so as an independent architect it was already clear that Wright was likely to become a specialist in designing houses. He had a flair for domestic architecture, and rich clients were beginning to seek him out to design new houses in the growing Chicago suburbs. But Wright's work in the early years was not all big houses for rich clients. He had to take on other work too, and no doubt was stimulated by the challenges it posed.

A spatial challenge
In the early 1890s, grain merchant Robert Roloson was looking to invest some of his money in property. He bought a group of four row houses set on three 25-foot (8-m) wide city lots on Chicago's South Calumet Avenue and employed Wright to remodel them. Here Wright faced the challenge of squeezing the accommodation into the narrow slices of land allocated for each house while also making a coherent street frontage.

The compact plans fit a lot in – dining rooms and kitchens at the back, drawing rooms and entrance halls at the front. And they pack all this in behind very imposing façades. Beneath each gable Wright placed rows of windows arranged in bold squares and set off with terracotta ornament. The resulting façades are clearly influenced by the Tudor Revival style that was popular in the late 19th century, but the main elements – the gables and groups of windows – are extra large, giving the frontage maximum impact on the street. The use of terracotta is very much in keeping with the kind of ornament favoured by Adler and Sullivan.

The Roloson Houses show that Wright could design buildings that fit into a city street but also make their mark. They suggest that his career could have gone a different way. Instead of designing detached suburban or country houses, he could have become a master of cityscape like Louis Sullivan, whose decorative style he imitated in the row house designs.

But Wright's career took a different turn. Although later in his life he drew up plans for cities that were never built, his inclination was towards houses that had more of a relationship to the ground – to buildings that reached out into their gardens or seemed to emerge organically from the earth. This was the kind of building for which Wright became famous.

Saved from the wrecking ball
By the time of the Second World War, when Wright's importance as a designer of large, one-off houses was firmly established, the Roloson Row Houses, so different from most of his output, were largely forgotten. In 1981 the buildings were gutted by fire, and it looked likely that they would be demolished. But fortunately they have been saved and restored. They do not look exactly as they did. For example, there was originally an ornamental wall with plump round balusters dividing the houses from the sidewalk. This has gone, but the façades are well cared for, and the buildings are designated as a Chicago landmark. They are a memorable tribute to the way the young Wright could take existing architectural ideas and make them his own.

ABOVE To the casual glance, these row houses do not look much like buildings by Wright, and his work on them was remodelling rather than designing from scratch. But the bold treatment of the windows, with the strong banding of stone, was a feature the architect would develop in some of his independent designs.

Romeo and Juliet Windmill

This small structure is a perfect example of the way Wright could take a familiar challenge – how to pump water from one place to another – and think it through afresh. Instead of a standard, commercially available wind pump, made of metal and with a limited life, the architect came up with a timber-framed structure, specially profiled to reduce wind load on the tower. The resulting board-clad Romeo and Juliet Windmill is both an efficient machine and a striking local landmark.

Location
Spring Green, Wisconsin

Client
Nell and Jane Lloyd Jones

Date
1896

Main material
Wood

Frank Lloyd Wright had two maternal aunts, Nell and Jane Lloyd Jones, who ran the Hillside Home School at Spring Green, Wisconsin. They were both unmarried, and had vowed to remain so in order to ensure the success of their school; and as they had no children of their own, those of their sister – especially young Frank – had a special place in their affections.

Wright versus the wind
In 1896 the sisters decided to improve the water supply at the school. A reservoir was dug and the sisters needed some way of pumping water from their artesian well into the reservoir. They were planning to buy a ready-made wind pump of the kind common on farms all over the USA and beyond, but then thought of their nephew: surely he would be able to come up with something more elegant, more interesting, and perhaps more effective too.

Wright rose to the challenge and soon a design was with the sisters' local builder, a man called Cramer. Wright called it the Romeo and Juliet Windmill because the plan was based on the coming together of two contrasting shapes, an octagon and a diamond. The idea was to face the sharp point of the diamond into the prevailing southwest wind, reducing wind resistance and making it less likely that the structure would be blown over. Otherwise, the mill is a simple design, a wooden frame clad originally with shingles (these were replaced with wooden siding in a later reconstruction). On top of the 60-foot (18-m) tower a large sail 14 feet (4 m) across harnesses the power of the wind to pump the water.

OPPOSITE The Romeo and Juliet Windmill manages the clever trick of at once standing out like a landmark and, with its wooden structure, looking at one with the background of bushes and trees. Above all, it is a far greater asset to the landscape than the alternative – a commercially available metal wind pump.

RIGHT A close-up of the windmill shows how the two components of the structure – the octagon and the diamond-shaped element – work together and are unified by the wooden cladding that they share. This covering, though a replacement for Wright's original shingles, is in keeping with the architect's ideas – he used similar siding on some of his houses.

Wright versus the sceptics
When Wright sent the plans of the windmill to Cramer there was an outcry. Cramer thought the proposed structure looked flimsy and forecast disaster. Wright's five uncles, local farmers, didn't like the look of the design either. Quickly the sisters telegraphed their nephew: 'CRAMER SAYS WINDMILL TOWER IS SURE TO FALL. ARE YOU SURE IT WILL STAND?' Wright replied in a letter, reassuring his aunts that the design of the tower was specifically meant to lower the wind resistance. The tower, he insisted, would outlast them all: Cramer should get on and build it. Wright admitted that he had never seen a design quite like this before, but he stood by the principle of the thing and by his ability to put the principle into practice.

The architect's confidence was well placed. Modestly, he claimed that the tower would last 25 years, pointing out that the alternative – an iron wind pump – would probably be worn out in less time. In fact, after repairs in 1938 and a rebuild in 1989–92, the mill is still standing. It remained Wright's companion when he brought his Taliesin Fellowship to Spring Green (see pages 100–101), steadily pumping water and acting as a platform for a loudspeaker, from which Wright broadcast music to his apprentices as they worked away in the surrounding fields.

It meant a lot to Wright to please his aunts and to prove his point against his uncles, who did not take his skills as an architect seriously. His father had found it difficult to do anything very well, or to hold down a job. Wright was going to be different, and he was going to show them all that being an architect was not simply a question of making attractive drawings of pretty buildings, but was about solving problems in theory and making the solutions work.

Frank Lloyd Wright Studio

Wright's studio complex at Oak Park is an extension to the house that he built for himself and his wife a few years earlier (see pages 12–15). The original house, with its big gable, was already an exercise in bold forms, but with the studio Wright went further, building an octagonal library and a drafting room also topped with an octagon. These structures added still stronger shapes, once more clad in brick and shingle, to this suburban block.

Location
Oak Park, Illinois
Client
The architect
Date
1897
Main materials
Wood, brick, shingle

By the late 1890s, Wright's practice was expanding and in 1895 he received an unusual commission: the Luxfer Prism Company ordered a number of designs featuring their patent window glass. This work proved lucrative, and Wright quickly found a way to spend the money it brought him – he decided to open another office, at his home in Oak Park. To house this new venture, he built an extension to the Oak Park house, pushing out into the garden an office, library and studio with their own entrance hall. The extension transformed the Oak Park house in a surprising and dramatic way.

New shapes and forms From the outside the studio complex looks quite unlike the rest of the house in shape and geometry, but it uses similar materials so that it is in harmony with the earlier structure. What strikes you first are the clearly defined shapes. In the middle is the entrance and office block, which is a low rectangle. To the right is the octagonal library; to the left the studio, the largest part of the complex. The studio is square, but is topped by another octagon, this time with windows all around which throw light down into the room below it. Although the site is small, Wright creates still more variety by breaking up the front wall, pulling the entrance forward a few feet and letting the front part of the octagonal library come still further forward, to create a feeling of depth. The façade throws interesting shadows, leaving a little space for trees and other planting, and is very satisfying. Anyone visiting the complex would be immediately impressed by its architect's ability to handle volumes and shapes.

Wright did not often get the chance to place non-rectangular structures on the grid of a city or suburb, but when he did, he delighted in the resulting interplay of shapes. The octagons at Oak Park, which take a step further the great bow windows on some of his early houses, also look forward to the time at the end of his career when he designed New York's Guggenheim Museum, imposing a vast spiral on a city block.

Light and space The heart of the complex is the large studio, a square room providing space for seven people to work around a central area that looks up toward a mezzanine and the octagon of light above. As in so many of his projects, Wright also designed the furniture and fittings, and used the cabinets and other pieces to divide up the space. The harmony resulting from the proportions, the care with which the room was divided into different workspaces and the overall use of wooden furniture designed by Wright must have been conducive to design work and drawing. But this harmony was not static. Wright was continually making changes and moving furniture around in attempts to improve the space.

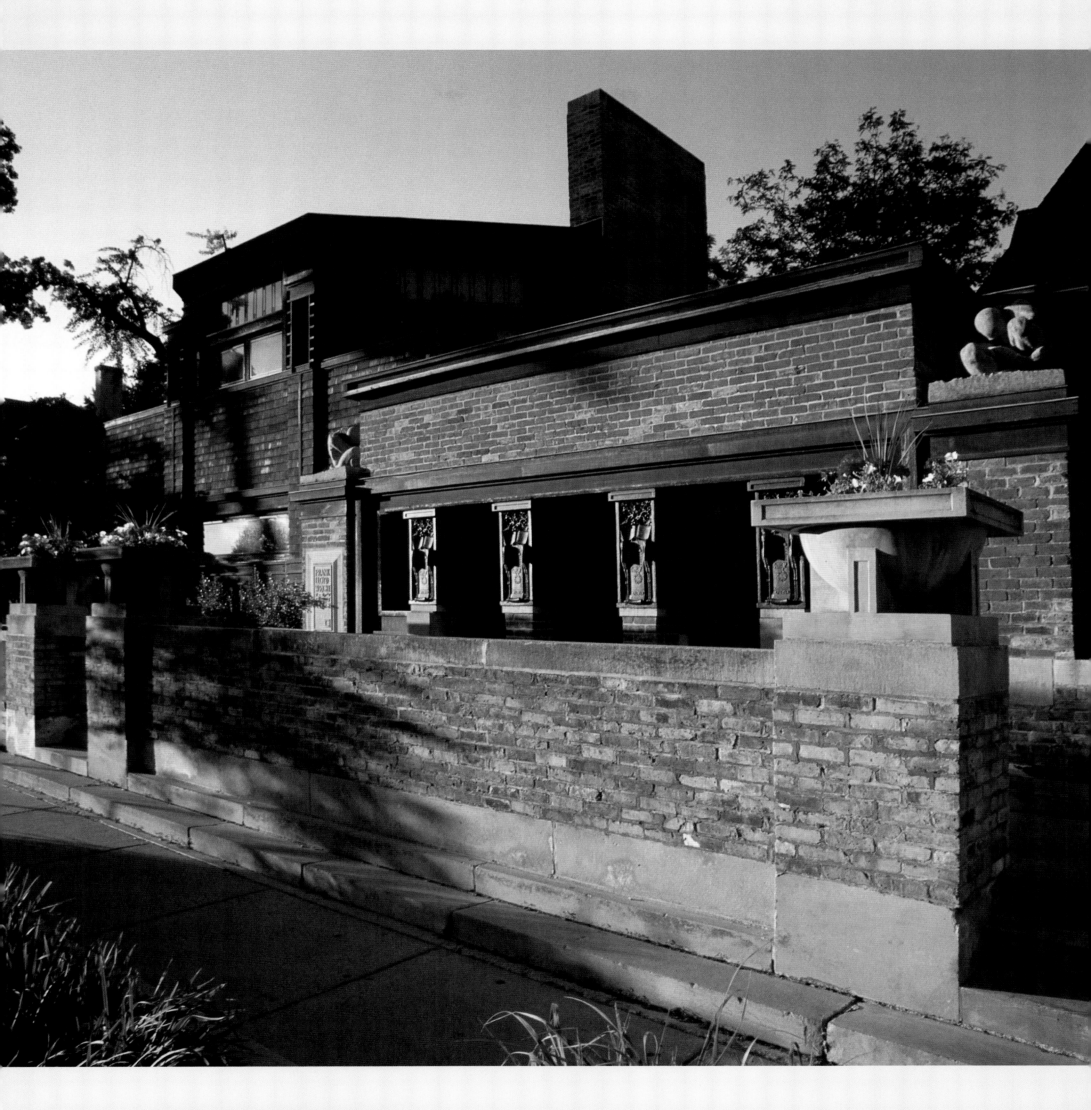

ABOVE In the studio extensions Wright added to his Oak Park house, he relished the opportunity to build in bold geometrical forms. The drafting room, topped with its octagonal lantern, is seen here beyond the more rectilinear entrance with its row of openings. Clients would have been immediately impressed by the inventiveness of the design.

The other rooms in the studio complex are smaller and more intimate. The library is a compact space. Its cupboards were not only for books but also for the architect's favourite objects and works of art, items that would inspire him when he was beginning to work out a design. Like the studio, the room is lit from above – this time both by strip windows around the tops of the walls and by a roof light – so that whatever objects Wright chose to arrange on the central table would be perfectly illuminated. The small office used by Wright himself was also top-lit, but was more informally arranged, with both window and skylight placed off-centre.

Wright kept on his 'downtown' office when the Oak Park complex was completed because he saw the advantage of having a city-centre base for business purposes. But the real work was done at Oak Park. In a printed announcement advertising the opening of the new studio, Wright welcomed visitors: 'Clients and those with kindred interest in architecture will also be welcomed to the suburban studio during business hours, where provision has been made for their reception and entertainment.' The Oak Park studio itself was a place where people could see, in both drawings and in the building itself, the Wright way of doing things.

Many buildings in one
It was a way of designing that Wright developed in future buildings. Although his later studios were very different in appearance, Wright used the idea of a series of semi-independent pavilions in them and in many of his houses. Carports, garages, service buildings and porches sweep out from main houses at different levels and on different alignments, rather as the studio and library do at Oak Park. And the breaks in walls enable trees and planting to 'wrap around' the buildings in interesting and picturesque ways, making it look as if the buildings are emerging from the landscape, a notion that became a favourite one for Wright.

OPPOSITE The octagonal library is top-lit with skylights in the ceiling and a strip of clerestory windows in the upper part of the walls. This arrangement of windows recalls an art gallery, and this is appropriate because the room housed a collection of prints and drawings as well as books.

BELOW This view shows how Wright designed the octagonal library extension so that it harmonized with the existing large-gabled house. He mirrored the small section of overhanging flat roof on the house with similar overhangs on the library at the same level. Above this overhang, the library's octagonal walls are covered with shingles, to reflect the shingles on the house gable.

Larkin Company Administration Building
30

Larkin Company Administration Building

The Larkin headquarters, an office block for a large company supplying a range of household goods, was one of the great buildings of the early 20th century. The façade was of heavy masonry, relieved only by a pair of tall pillars, but at the side there were big windows to fill the workspaces with light. Inside there was a huge top-lit atrium, surrounded by balconies with scores of desks. This layout was subsequently imitated in countless office buildings, though few of its imitators were as grand and monumental.

Location
Buffalo, New York

Client
Larkin Company

Date
1903 (demolished 1950)

Main material
Brick

OPPOSITE Large masses of masonry gave the street façade of the Larkin Administration Building a monumental quality, which the architect hoped would still look impressive if the walls were blackened by industrial pollution. Although there were some windows in the centre part of the frontage, they gave little hint of how light the building was inside.

RIGHT Skylights illuminated the vast atrium of the building, throwing into relief the carved decoration on the upper parts of the columns. The balcony fronts bore uplifting inscriptions, reminding the Larkin Company's employees of the virtues of such qualities as economy, industry and cooperation.

'Nearly every technological innovation used today was suggested in the Larkin Building in 1904.' Frank Lloyd Wright was rarely modest about his buildings but this time he was not far wrong. The list is staggering: air conditioning, double-glazed plate-glass windows, glass doors, built-in steel desks, hung lavatory walls that you could clean beneath, wall-mounted WCs, a built-in vacuum-cleaning system, sub-floor electric lighting. All these features of the Larkin Building were widely copied by other architects in the following decades.

The Larkin Company had begun in 1875 as a soap manufacturer but by the beginning of the 20th century it had expanded into groceries, furniture and household goods. They sold the goods they made by mail order, cutting out the middleman. The business boomed, and the company needed new offices.

A landmark building

Wright gave them a building to be proud of, a building that made a mark on its Buffalo street, stood out from the huge Larkin factories and warehouses behind it, and provided an efficient and agreeable environment for its workers. This was a combination that appealed to Larkin and his fellow directors, who were happy to invest some of their wealth in a building that would be pleasant for their employees.

Outside, the Larkin Building was like a fortress – a great cliff of a building in dark brick, on five floors. Tall, massive and brooding, this exterior looked somewhat forbidding, but it was also practical. Wright chose the dark brick because he knew that the walls would soon become soiled with city grime, and the dark colour would take the scars of pollution better than paler masonry.

Both light and enlightened

The interior was a rather different story. For a start, it was very light, making it an inviting place in which to work, something that appealed to the Larkin bosses, who valued their workers' welfare. A huge central atrium was topped with a skylight, illuminating the workspaces on the first floor below and on the balconies that lined this huge space. The wall cladding, a cream-coloured glazed brick that could be easily cleaned, increased the lightness. In all, it made a comfortable workplace for the 1,800 administrative workers of the Larkin empire.

This was just as well, because the building went $62,000 over budget. The Larkins were shocked, but soon realized that the landmark headquarters they now had was worth much more than this in publicity value. An illustration of the building was printed on their letterhead, and became an effective symbol of the firm.

The Larkin Company did well until the Great Depression, but, like many, did not recover from the economic disaster. The building was sold in1943 and demolished in 1950. Now the innovative design of Wright's early masterpiece can be appreciated only through photographs.

Unity Temple

The church where Wright worshipped every Sunday was always a special building to him and he designed it to stand out on the street. At the front of the building, plain walls are pierced by high windows and topped by flat overhanging roofs. At each corner, bulky square stair towers flank the main façades. This is a revolutionary design for a church, all the more so because it is built in poured concrete, an unusual but trendsetting material for a public building in the early 1900s.

In 1905 the Unitarian church in Oak Park was destroyed in a fire. The congregation straight away began to plan a replacement for the old building, which had been an old-fashioned Gothic Revival church. There were two problems. First, just $40,000 was available to pay for the new building. Second, it was difficult to decide what kind of building everyone wanted, and who should design it.

The church and the people
Some members of the congregation wanted to hold a competition to choose the best design, but the building committee that had been formed threw out this idea. The pastor, Dr Rodney F. Johonnot, liked the idea of a traditional North American colonial church, a white building with a spire, but the committee chose Wright as architect and Wright's ideas were a very long way from traditional. He did not like the idea of a spire. 'Why build a conventional church, with a spire pointing literally to heaven?' he said. He preferred instead the notion that God's kingdom was present in the gathering of worshipping people.

Wright planned a church that would look like no previous place of worship, a building that even at over a hundred years old still looks rather surprising in its leafy surroundings. It is a tribute to the congregation – and perhaps the persuasive powers of the architect and his friend on the building committee, Charles E. Roberts – that it got built at all.

Location
Oak Park, Illinois

Client
The congregation of Unity Church

Date
1905

Main material
Poured concrete

RIGHT This exterior view in strong sunlight shows how the temple's walls resolve into a composition of planes and forms as ordered as a constructivist painting. The flat roofs, slightly projecting cornices and decorative elements are designed to cast shadows in the sun to relieve the effect of the expanses of pale concrete.

LEFT The skylights are glazed with stained glass in simple abstract patterns of rectangles and squares, each square deeply recessed for added shadows and visual textures. The colour of the glass is just strong enough to give a warm glow to the light inside the building.

One challenge of the project was the site, which had a narrow frontage but went back a long way. Wright turned this to his advantage, placing the church, Unity Temple itself, at the front, and building another linked structure, Unity House, at the back to accommodate the lay activities of the congregation.

Unity Temple, like many other churches, is a cruciform structure, but it does not look cross-shaped from the outside because Wright placed at the corners square stair towers that rise almost to the top of the building. These towers combine with the plain walls, high windows and flat roofs to make an astonishing composition for a church, with little ornament except for the ornate uprights in the windows, which have reminded many of the decorations on Mayan temples.

A new use for concrete
What is more, the church is built of concrete, and the walls were made by pouring the concrete on site. This method became commonplace in the later 20th century, but was little short of revolutionary in 1905. Only one or two previous buildings had been constructed in this way, and no one had built a church like this: Unity Temple was America's first public building constructed of exposed concrete. Many contemporaries found the resulting wall surfaces ugly. As Wright's biographer Brendan Gill puts it, 'Many parishioners prayed for ivy and were happy when ivy came.'

ABOVE By running red and black lines around
many elements – pulpit, light fittings and balcony
fronts as well as walls – Wright brought a formal
unity to the interior of the church. In a space
without lavish images or rich decoration, Wright
created a peaceful atmosphere that fosters
contemplation, reading and prayer.

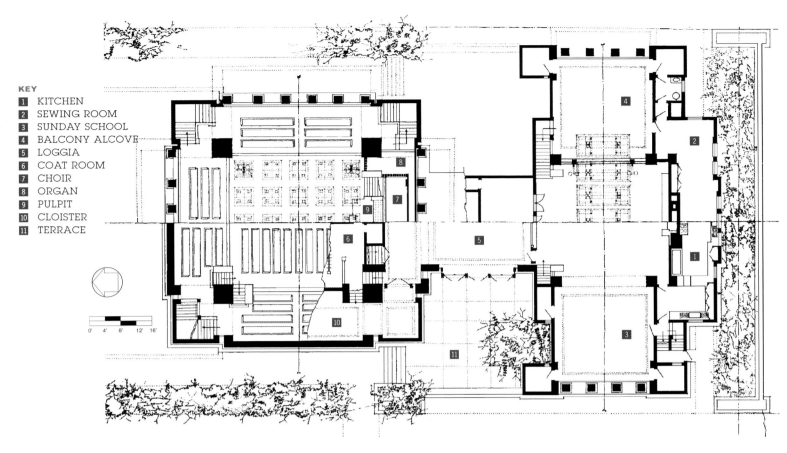

Unity Temple (church) plan, composite of three levels

ABOVE The plan of Unity Temple shows clearly how Wright divided the building into two sections, linked by a central entrance loggia. To the left is the church itself – different sections of the plan indicate the long pews and the square skylights above. To the right is Unity House, with its spaces for the Sunday school and other activities.

Order and light

Inside Unity Temple itself there is more warmth and beauty. This does not come from ornament, which is restrained, but from proportions and light. The proportions of the interior derive from a carefully worked-out series of squares, cubes and double cubes, creating a sense of balance and order. The light comes mainly from above – from a grid of square skylights and strips of high clerestory windows. There is stained glass in these windows, but its colour is very restrained – just enough, in the main, to give a warm tinge of amber to the incoming light. Although Wright rejected the pastor's idea of a church with a spire pointing to heaven, he was happy to let the light from the sky be drawn into the room, and to make it feel like warm sunlight even on a cloudy day. So warm and harmonious is the interior that it is easy to forget, given Wright's extensive use of wooden trim and his specially designed light fittings and furniture, that even here there is a lot of exposed concrete.

The church is a compact space. When seated for worship, no one is far from the pulpit and everyone is close together. The feeling of community is important, and is emphasized too in the other main part of the building, Unity House, which is conceived along more domestic lines, with a fireplace near which parishioners could assemble for meetings, or children could gather for Sunday school.

Wright took great pains with the design of Unity Temple. He said in his autobiography that he went through 34 different studies for the building before he reached the final design. When they got used to their unusual church, the parishioners were grateful, and Unity Temple remains one of Wright's most original and best loved buildings.

RIGHT Special care was paid to the light fittings. They are conceived as a coming together of spheres and cubes that branch out from supports dropping down from the ceiling. Even the tops of the cubic fittings, with their patterns of squares unseen by most of the congregation, were treated with great attention to detail.

Midway Gardens

Like the European pleasure gardens of the 18th and 19th centuries, Midway Gardens was a place where people could go to eat, drink and be entertained, indoors and out. It consisted of a series of walls and buildings, mostly elaborately decorated with cast concrete designs and with specially commissioned sculptures, and from every angle it presented to the viewer an enticing array of pavilions, roofs and towers, as if the Aztecs had adapted their architecture to entertainment and play.

Location
Chicago, Illinois

Client
Edward C. Waller Jr

Date
1913 (demolished 1929)

Main materials
Brick, patterned concrete block

In 1910, Wright went on a visit to Europe. He had always been a follower of the theatre and had an interest in music, and he was impressed by the way in which, in countries such as Germany, the arts were made part of outdoor entertainment spaces such as beer gardens and pleasure parks. In 1913 he was given the opportunity to create an American version of this kind of venue, when he was commissioned to design Midway Gardens in Chicago.

High and low culture meet
Wright's concept was to bring sophistication to the beer garden by combining eating and drinking with high-quality music. He also wanted the experience to be quintessentially American, so he evolved a decorative style all his own, that drew partly on the art of the ancient pre-Columbian cultures of Mexico.

Midway Gardens combined a five-tiered garden and bandstand with such indoor facilities as a club, a tavern, a restaurant and a dance hall. It was large – filling a 600-foot (185-m) square city block – and lavishly decorated with a series of sculptures, which Wright designed in collaboration with the sculptor Alfonso Iannelli. Their figure sculptures, which became known as Sprites, held various abstract geometric forms such as a cube, an octagon and a triangle. These shapes had symbolic associations for Wright, and – so the architect believed – embodied a kind of geometric 'spell power'.

By combining symbolic sculptures with dance floors, beer-drinking with fine architecture, and a casino with good music, the gardens presented a rich mixture of American culture. In the gardens was another, visually appealing contrast: between the prolific mass-produced concrete – often cast to make decorative surfaces – and the striking, hand-made sculptures of Iannelli. At many levels, Wright was bringing high and low culture together in what he saw as a very democratic and American way.

A grand opening
All the signs were that it would prove a success. The opening took place on 27 June 1914, the day before the assassination of Austrian Archduke Franz Ferdinand in Sarajevo began the train of events that led to the First World War. Wright described the scene in his autobiography: 'In a scene unforgettable to all who attended, the architectural scheme and color, form, light, and sound had come alive. Thousands of beautifully dressed women and tuxedoed men thronged the scene. And this scene came upon the beholders as a magic spell. All there moved and spoke as if in a dream. They believed it must be one. Yes. Chicago marveled, acclaimed, approved. And Chicago came back and did the same, marveling again and again and again.'

Dispute and decline
The prospects for the gardens looked good, but shadows fell over the success. Wright became embroiled in a dispute with Iannelli over the way the sculptor was credited. Wright described the Sprites as 'designed by Frank Lloyd Wright, executed by A. Janelli', which reduced the sculptor's role and added insult to injury by spelling his name incorrectly. Iannelli insisted that he had a key creative role; Wright claimed that the basic ideas were his own and that Iannelli's role was more that of a craftsman than a creative artist.

But more damaging than this dispute was that the owners, who had lacked sufficient ready capital to build the gardens, found that the takings after opening were not enough for them to pay their way. By 1916 they were in receivership, and the gardens passed into other hands. They declined until Prohibition put an end to the kind of entertainment offered there, and they were finally demolished in 1929. A unique masterpiece of architecture and garden planning was lost to Chicago and the world.

OPPOSITE Sculptures by Iannelli guarded the street frontages of the gardens complex, looking down from plinths on top of carefully crafted brick walls. Posters advertise the fact that the gardens are now open, their proprietors no doubt hopeful that a large audience would gather there to be entertained. Sadly, after the first rush of interest, the hope was not fulfilled.

ABOVE Automobiles throng in front of one of the flat-roofed pavilions that made up the main structures in Midway Gardens. These pavilions, similar to those at Tokyo's Imperial Hotel, were covered with abstract decoration, which both architect and client felt was appropriate to buildings associated with a venue devoted to pleasure and entertainment.

Imperial Hotel

Tokyo's Imperial Hotel, in a prominent position near the Imperial Palace, was one of Frank Lloyd Wright's largest projects. With its long wings of bedrooms and its large public rooms – often encrusted with ornament, like the triple-height grand lobby – it was one of the Japanese capital's landmark buildings. The hotel was all the more remarkable because Wright found a way of making it earthquake-proof.

Location
Tokyo, Japan

Client
Hotel management on behalf of Japanese imperial family

Date
1914–22
(demolished 1968)

Main materials
Poured concrete, Oya stone (soft lava block)

Japan – its art, culture and architecture – fascinated Frank Lloyd Wright. He visited the country, collected Japanese prints, and analysed the country's buildings. He felt that the Japanese house, typically grounded in the landscape and using local materials, represented an ideal way to build, a way more 'modern' than contemporary Western architecture because its form grew directly from function and materials. So when Wright was given the chance to design a major building in the Japanese capital, Tokyo, he was enthusiastic, and ended up spending several years in the country seeing the job through.

A challenging project
Although both the plan of the hotel and its decorative details in some ways derive from Midway Gardens, this was a highly complex building that took months of planning, as Wright developed his vision of a building that would provide the visitor with a host of visual delights. Wright took pains to make the hotel an enjoyable place to stay. Not for him the broiler-house uniformity of modern hotel design: almost every room was different from all the others.

The earthquake threat
But the challenge that exercised Wright more than any other was how to cope with the threat of earthquakes. Wright examined the geology of the site and found that it did not help him by offering any kind of solid support. Beneath the topsoil were 60 feet (18 m) of subsoil, with no bedrock within reach. Wright described it graphically as 'eight feet of cheese-like soil that overlay … liquid mud'.

The solution seemed to be to 'float' the building on the mud rather than trying to find some hard foundation for it. In order to do this, Wright designed a series of concrete 'pins' that sank 9 feet (3 m) into the soil. The floor slabs of the building were supported on these pins and cantilevered out from them. The idea was that the building above could move about independently of these pins, coming back to rest on them again once an earthquake was over. In addition, the building was laid out in relatively small sections, with expansion joints in between.

Wright's clients were far from confident that this construction system would work. They insisted that the architect stay in Tokyo for the entire period of construction, and so Wright remained in Tokyo until 1921, watching the building rise, and fending off doubts about his construction methods. He was saved by an earth tremor that hit the hotel when it was under construction. The building shook but stayed in one piece – or rather in its various, independently shifting component pieces – and Wright won new respect as a result.

Telling details
Wright's time in Tokyo meant that he oversaw all the details of the building – the fittings and fixtures, which he had designed, were made and installed under his supervision, making the vast complex a very pure Frank Lloyd Wright building. The overwhelming impression of the ornament is that of a Mayan temple, but the scale of the guest rooms, doors, fittings and spaces is smaller, and more Japanese. Peter Blake, a writer who saw the building, described the attention to scale in his book on Wright: '… in some of the rooms the glazed doors leading out to little balconies are hardly more than five feet high; elsewhere, windows overlooking gardens and courts are so low that one must get down on all fours to enjoy the view.'

The ultimate test
The acid test of the building came dramatically in the great earthquake of 1923. Large parts of the capital were flattened, 100,000 people lost their lives, but out of the confusion Wright received a telegram from the hotel's chairman, Baron Okyra: 'HOTEL STANDS UNDAMAGED AS MONUMENT OF YOUR GENIUS HUNDREDS OF HOMELESS PROVIDED FOR BY PERFECTLY MAINTAINED SERVICE CONGRATULATIONS'. The Imperial Hotel lasted another 40 years, and was finally demolished in 1968. It fell in the end not because of earth tremors but because of the pressures of economics, when developers saw they could make money out of a high-rise building on the site.

FRANK LLOYD WRIGHT'S first great creative period lasted from about 1901 to 1910. This was the decade during which he designed a stunning series of buildings known as the 'Prairie Houses'. These houses are not on the Prairies, but would be at home there – they are low houses with strong horizontal emphasis in the design; they seem to reach out into the landscape, and have many porches and balconies, allowing house and landscape to merge; they have views out in many different directions; and they have cantilevered roofs that, like the porches, stretch out to embrace the garden.

Wright planned many of his Prairie Houses using a grid. He had seen this method used in Japanese architecture, where the floor plan of a house would be based on multiples of the standard 6 foot x 3 foot (2 m x 1 m) tatami mat. Wright used grids (sometimes of rectangles, sometimes of squares) in a similar way: the size of the grid would determine not only the dimensions of the floor, but also the size of windows and the distance between elements such as wall timbers. It was a useful design discipline but could also save money when based, as it sometimes was, on the size of standard building components.

Although based on squares, however, Prairie Houses were rarely square in plan. Many had cross-shaped footprints, or plans based on the 'pinwheel' (a kind of cross with offset arms). In a typical cross plan, each arm would house a main room (living room, dining room, kitchen and entry, for example), while the hearth, the heart of all Wright's houses, was placed at the centre. A particular advantage of this kind of plan was that a room occupying a complete arm of the cross had views in three directions, making it light, sun-filled, and – crucially for Wright – giving a range of views of the garden and landscape. This unity of inside and outside, of house and site, was a key feature of what Wright came to call 'organic architecture'.

THE PRAIRIE
HOUSE AND
BEYOND

Willits House

The Ward Willits House, in the Chicago suburb of
Highland Park, is a revolutionary building. With its cruciform
plan, interpenetrating internal spaces and overhanging roofs,
it is quite different from other houses being built at this time.
In particular, its horizontal, ground-hugging form is the hallmark
of a kind of house – the Prairie House, as it came to be called
– that was soon to make Wright famous.

Location
Highland Park, Illinois

Client
Ward Winfield Willits

Date
1901

Main materials
Wood, plaster, glass,
steel

Ward Winfield Willits was Vice President of Adams and Westlake,
a Chicago brass foundry. One of the firm's ex-employees, Orlando
Giannini, was later hired by Wright to work on decorative glazing, and
it may be that Giannini introduced the architect to his former boss.
In 1901 Willits commissioned Wright to design his new house. The
Prairie House style, with which Wright would become so closely
identified, was the result.

The key feature of Wright's Prairie Houses is a strong horizontal
emphasis. Wright identified this form of building with the ground itself,
and above all the American ground. As Peter Blake has written:
'Horizontality was Wright's response not only to the earth and to the things that grew out of it, but also to
the great spaces of America.' And the great spaces meant the Prairies. These houses were American in
another way, too. Their free planning, with interior rooms merging with one another, gave the inhabitants
room to wander around in a space that seemed almost limitless (and which often merged, via porches and
loggias, with the garden). Prairie Houses did not have to be on the Prairies – many of them are sited in
Chicago suburbs – but their generous proportions still manage to suggest the vast open spaces of the
American Midwest.

The first Prairie House
For many, the Ward Willits House is the first of the Prairie Houses.
Its plan extends into the garden in four directions, radiating out from the central hearth. Looking from
the main garden front, the centre wing, containing the large living room, protrudes forwards, with a strip
of five French windows opening on to a terrace. The wing to the left houses the dining room, which
looks forwards (with more French windows), backwards and sideways to a long porch sheltered by a
continuation of the dining-room roof. To the right, the entrance hall opens off a porte cochère (a kind
of drive-in porch), which balances the porch off the dining room. To the rear of the house, a fourth
wing projects; this contains servants' rooms and the kitchen, which also has views across the garden.

All the main rooms have plenty of windows, and the plan allows the two main spaces – the living
and dining rooms – to have windows looking in three different directions. The plan is an object lesson
in merging indoors and outdoors, and Wright's drawings reflect this, including as they do the positions
of pathways, drives, and trees and other planting.

A wooden frame
The structure that makes all this possible is very American too. A
quintessentially North American form of house construction uses a wooden frame, a method of building
that was appreciated for its cheap materials and the ease with which it could be assembled. The Ward
Willits residence is hardly a typical frame house, but its structure is supported on a wooden frame, and
the size of the windows and doorways is dictated by the gaps between the framework. Not all the
framework of the Willits House is visible from the outside – much of it is covered with the pale plaster

LEFT This frontal view shows how the house is arranged
in projecting wings. Pushing forward towards the garden
is the wing containing the living room, which opens on to
a terrace. The dining-room wing is just visible to the left.
The wing to the right accommodates the entrance hall, its
low roof extending further right to cover a porte cochère.

that gives the walls their solid-looking quality – but the way the uprights between the windows are left visible emphasizes this frame structure, and, inside, visible ceiling timbers also add to the 'frame effect'.

To cap it all, there are Wright's trademark overhanging roofs. They are shallow, hipped roofs, much less showy than the upturned roofs of the Dana House (see pages 46–49), and they embrace the whole structure, including the porches, providing shelter and also shade for the upper windows. The brown tiles pick up the colouring of the timbers, lending a muted harmony to the exterior.

The effect of light on the exterior was also something that preoccupied Wright. His use of a grid of brown timbers with pale plaster gave the walls a strong, articulated character. The use of coloured glass and intricate patterns of leading in the windows enhanced the effect. Large, uninterrupted expanses of plate glass look black in natural light and add little to a façade. By breaking them up into leaded panes, Wright made them look more 'alive' in the sun, which catches the leading and illuminates the tiny differences in surface caused by the leading, making the windows glitter.

With its warm, woody interiors, welcoming hearths and happy relationship with the surrounding garden, the Willits House was a success. Ward Willits and his wife remained friends with Wright, accompanying him and his wife on their first trip to Japan in 1905. But more than this, the house was Wright's first true Prairie House, giving him a set of design solutions that he could evolve in numerous other houses in the next ten years or so, some of which were among his greatest buildings.

RIGHT Leaded glass – 'art glass', as it became known – arranged in abstract geometrical designs, with restrained use of colour, plays a key part in the design of the Willits House. Wright laid out the design with most of the decorative elements close to the edges of the window, so that they did not interrupt the view out.

LEFT Part of the living room shows the characteristic Wright combination of materials and colours – pale ceilings broken up with dark beams above, a rich wood floor below. Natural materials such as wood always appealed to Wright, who came to see them as essential in his organic architecture.

BELOW The cruciform plan of the Willits House is divided into living, dining, entrance and service wings. The geometry of the rectangular wings is made more interesting with the use of pointed and three-sided bays, as well as by vistas into the various porches, terraces and verandas.

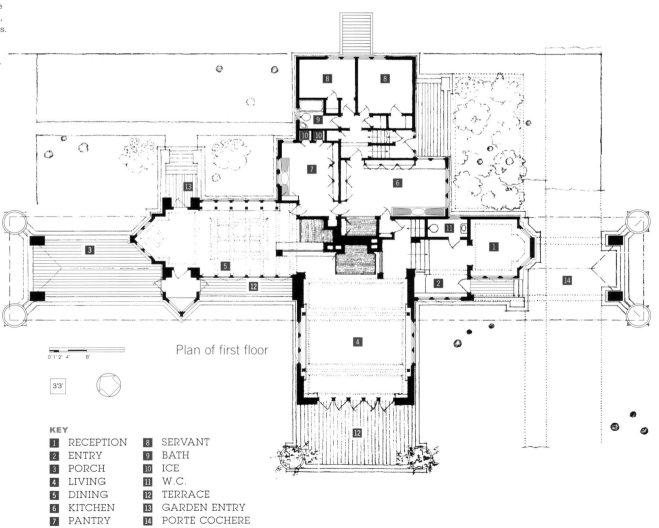

Plan of first floor

0' 1' 2' 4'   8'

3'3'

KEY

1	RECEPTION	**8**	SERVANT
2	ENTRY	**9**	BATH
3	PORCH	**10**	ICE
4	LIVING	**11**	W.C.
5	DINING	**12**	TERRACE
6	KITCHEN	**13**	GARDEN ENTRY
7	PANTRY	**14**	PORTE COCHERE

ABOVE This pointed bay provides a glazed link between the conservatory (left) and the gallery (right) of the Susan Lawrence Dana House. The generous windows and high-quality masonry, with provision for planting in the coping, are typical Wright features, but the unusual upturned pitched roofs give the house its unique character.

Dana House

One of Wright's largest houses, the residence he designed for Susan Lawrence Dana in Springfield, Illinois, is a dazzling essay in brickwork, coloured glass and overhanging pitched roofs. Based on a cross-shaped plan, its many wings, bays and overhangs create a complex building that beautifully exploits the effects of light and shade. Trailing plants spilling over ledges, and balconies enhance the effect and bring house and garden harmoniously together.

Location
Springfield, Illinois
Client
Susan Lawrence Dana
Date
1902
Main materials
Brick

Susan Lawrence Dana was an ideal client for Wright. A widow who had inherited a huge fortune, including the income from some silver mines in the Rockies, she was also a keen collector of Japanese paintings and prints. At the beginning of the 20th century, she decided to remodel the family home, a mansion in the Italianate style in the rich district of Springfield known as 'Aristocracy Hill'. When she found Wright, she knew she had the man for the job.

A convivial house

The job, though, expanded as Wright's ideas multiplied and his client's enthusiasm grew. Far from a remodelling, the project became an almost completely new house with a few traces of original rooms hidden away at its heart. Susan Lawrence Dana wanted a big house in which she could entertain on a lavish scale, and that is what she got.

So the main rooms are on the grand scale. The double-height dining room contains a table that can seat 40. There is a large vaulted gallery, also a high room, to house Lawrence Dana's art collection and accommodate large social gatherings. The library, another big room, was also used for entertaining.

What is striking about these rooms, apart from their sheer size, is the way they connect with one another. There are no corridors in the house; instead, one space leads to another, divided from its neighbours by large double doors that can be thrown enticingly open, so that visitors appreciate how the spaces link together. This makes the building a highly social house, one in which the client's parties, sometimes attended by hundreds of guests, could take over the entire main floor. This kind of planning, with merging spaces opening up a series of attractive views, was increasingly used by Wright.

RIGHT Several of the spaces in the Dana House, like this reception room, rise to double height, making them ideal for grand occasions such as the large parties the original owner often hosted. As usual in Wright's houses, the focus here is on a large fireplace, in this case made of carefully laid brickwork.

Another feature of the interiors was that everything was designed by Wright. There are still more than a hundred pieces of furniture in light oak, ranging from the vast dining table to small chairs and easels in the gallery, designed by the architect. This was the way he liked to work, creating the whole environment, and many of his houses contain his own tables and chairs. But rarely did he have a client so rich, or so indulgent, as Susan Lawrence Dana.

Working with light
The play of natural light is a hugely important aspect of any house, and Wright, as always, paid special attention to the windows. His plan helped him here – the Dana House is roughly cruciform, and the cross-shaped layout means that many rooms have windows in two or even three walls, so that light floods the interior from all directions. Intricate arrangements of glazing bars and lavish use of coloured glass take full advantage of this light. The amount of glass in the building is truly staggering – there are more than 400 windows, skylights, doors and other glazed items such as lamps. Wright designed them all, many with variations of a sumac tree motif, some with flowers such as purple aster and golden rod. Their colours tend to bring out the warm, golden tones of the sunlight entering the house.

Exterior details
The building is just as stunning from the outside. The main walls are built in pale brick, so that the first impression is of a house that sits on massive chunks of masonry. But Wright treated this brickwork in a very special way, instructing the builders to hollow out the pointing of the horizontal masonry joints, while leaving the vertical joints flush with the brick surface. This means that you hardly notice the vertical joints, whereas the horizontals cast a strong shadow, making the brickwork 'read' as a series of narrow horizontal bands. This banding effect is also used in the brickwork that surrounds the main, arched doorway of the house, creating an impression rather like the 'Roman' brickwork used in other houses by Wright. It is an object lesson in how careful attention to a simple detail can transform the appearance of a building.

The roofs are beautifully designed, too. They seem to hover above the walls, because they are separated from the masonry piers by windows and sections of wall set back from the main building line. The roofs overhang generously and are also turned up slightly at the edges. This touch recalls traditional Japanese buildings. No doubt it appealed to Mrs Dana for this reason, but it also adds to the effect of the roofs being airborne and detached from the main structure.

Susan Lawrence Dana was pleased with her house and lived in it until the late 1920s, when her fortune declined and the time for grand parties was over. She retired to a small cottage in the grounds and eventually the house was bought by the publisher Charles C. Thomas, who sold it at much less than its market price to the State of Illinois. Restored in the late 1980s, it is preserved as one of Wright's greatest and most complete houses.

RIGHT Another of the grand, double-height rooms in the Dana House is the dining room. It has a huge vaulted ceiling – a feature Wright had developed on a smaller scale in his own Oak Park house – and is furnished with distinctive high-backed dining chairs designed, like much of the furniture in the house, by Wright himself. At one end, the lower level of the room continues into a semi-circular breakfast nook with built-in seating, which can be seen at the bottom of the picture.

Plan of first floor

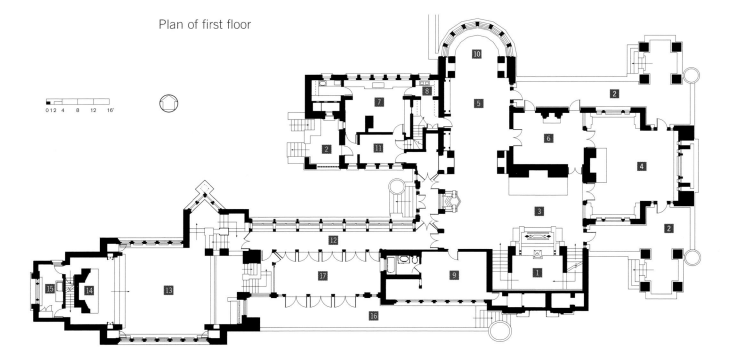

0 1 2 4   8   12   16'

KEY
1 ENTRY
2 PORCH
3 RECEPTION
4 LIVING
5 DINING
6 PARLOUR (OLD HOUSE LIBRARY)
7 KITCHEN
8 PANTRY
9 BED
10 BREAKFAST NOOK
11 SERVANTS' DINING
12 CONSERVATORY
13 GALLERY
14 ALCOVE
15 SERVANTS' KITCHEN
16 SOUTH TERRACE
17 ENCLOSED PORCH

ABOVE The Dana House is one of Wright's largest. As well as the expected collection of generously proportioned living rooms – including the parlour that remains from the original house on the site – there is a large west wing. This consists of a long conservatory and porch leading to the gallery.

Gerts Summer Cottage

A modest cottage in the woods, the Gerts Summer Cottage shows how much care Frank Lloyd Wright could devote to even the smallest holiday home. Where many architects would have been content to produce a simple four-square cabin, Wright designed a house carefully perched on a hillside, entered through a unique porch on a bridge above a creek. The small wooden house is perfectly integrated with its setting among the trees.

Location
Whitehall, Michigan

Client
George and Mary Gerts

Date
1902

Main materials
Wood

Many of Wright's rich clients had more than one home, and sometimes Wright, having pleased a client once with a successful house design, won a commission to design a second home for the same person. These cottages or summer houses were often much simpler than their owners' main houses. They were places where their owners could get back to nature, and enjoy a slightly more sophisticated version of life in a cabin in the woods or by a lake. A number were timber-framed buildings clad in boards, a form of construction that was both inexpensive and appropriate in a country setting.

Two outstanding examples are the cottages Wright built in Whitehall, Michigan, for the father and son George and Walter Gerts. The cottage built for George Gerts and his wife Mary, to whom Wright addressed his plans, is especially appealing. It stands among trees by a creek, and Wright was obviously inspired by the site to produce a striking design. The main body of the house stands on the slope above the creek; but it is entered from the other side of the water over a bridge, which Wright roofed to create a porch. As you enter, there are views of the trees and stream. At the end of the bridge, the large living area extends either side, while the bedrooms are sited on an upper floor to the rear.

Working with wood

The timber structure dominates the house – only the chimney is of masonry and the tiled roofs are low in pitch so they do not dominate the building in the way they do in many of the architect's larger houses. This timberwork is a very traditional North American form of construction, used since colonial times and used in Wright's Romeo and Juliet Windmill. The underlying framework is made of vertical 4-inch x 4-inch (10-cm x 10-cm) posts placed 3 feet (1 m) apart. They can be seen clearly between the windows, and they also appear inside between the plasterwork. These uprights are tied together by horizontal 1-foot (30-cm) wide board siding, which braces and gives strength to the underlying timber framework. To cover the joints between these boards, Wright specified narrow battens to be nailed over them. This has the strong visual effect of emphasizing the horizontal lines, producing the impression, typical in Wright's houses, of a low-slung structure that hugs the ground.

The effect is very modern because of the strips of windows all the way along the porch and around the living room, above which the roofs seem to float. In the right light the glass reflects the leaves and branches of the surrounding trees, emphasizing the integration of house and surroundings.

Looking to the future

The house and landscape are further linked by the porch-bridge. Building over water like this must have appealed to Wright, and years later, when he built the great house Fallingwater for Edgar Kaufmann (see pages 102–105), he seized the opportunity to balance the house above a waterfall. The seeds of this much more famous house are planted in this modest Michigan summer residence.

There is another way in which Wright was storing up ideas for the future in this project. Although he built lavish houses for rich clients all the way through his career, Wright had a strong social conscience, and wanted to apply his ideas and designs to smaller, less costly houses for ordinary Americans, without losing the organic, free-flowing feeling of his larger projects. Buildings like this summer cottage enabled him to experiment and to discover ways in which he could create a stunning house with relatively meagre means. Economical timber structures like the Gerts Cottage, so attractive to an architect devoted to 'organic' architecture, provided the key to these designs.

OPPOSITE With its entrance-bridge across the stream, its pale blue wooden siding, and its long, low profile, the Gerts Summer Cottage is an outstanding example of a house artfully designed for its site. Although a small house, it is a good example of the architect thinking out a design from first principles and coming up with an original solution.

Darwin Martin House

The Darwin Martin House is a Prairie House on the grandest of scales.
All the by-now familiar Wright hallmarks – overhanging roofs, porches, bands
of windows, cruciform plan – are there, but on a vast scale. The huge porch that
leads off the main living room is bigger than the living room itself. The pergola
that links the house with the garage is longer than the whole house. It is a big
house for a big businessman.

Location
Buffalo, New York
Client
Darwin D. Martin
Date
1904
Main materials
Brick

Darwin D. Martin and his brother W.E. Martin were the owners of Martin and Martin, manufacturers
of E-Z Stove Polish of Chicago. Their metal polish ('World Beater' was one slogan on the letterhead,
'Does it easy' another) made them a lot of money, and at the same time as he was designing the Larkin
Building, the Martins commissioned Wright to build them a new factory in Chicago, so that they could
make still more.

A grand project Darwin Martin, a meticulous businessman who was careful with his figures
and aware of the benefits of getting things right, was very impressed by Wright, and also hired the
architect to build him a new home – a grand 'Prairie House' in Buffalo, New York. Before long, this
commission had expanded to include a second, smaller house in one corner of the same plot, to be
occupied by the sister and brother-in-law of Martin's wife (see pages 56–57). The complete job was
a very big project and Wright was convinced that he could build the Martins their perfect house.

Martin was impressed, admiring Wright's designs and identifying with the architect's crusade to get every detail right, no matter how many revisions to the plans were needed. But all this meant that the project went slowly. This began to frustrate Martin's wife, and when the budget started to increase, Martin began to express his worries too.

Counting the cost

By the time the houses were finished, they probably cost more than $100,000, several times what Martin had originally intended to spend. To give an idea of what this meant, the small Prairie House design that Wright had based his original plans on was for a house costing around $7,000. The Martins would have expected to pay several times this for their much bigger residence, but not more than 14 times as much. They were stung, but they saw the project through.

Martin and Wright exchanged mountains of letters about the design and the progress of the building, and Martin confided despairingly to his brother about Wright's methods. But Martin seemed to think that problems like the ones he was having were inevitable because of Wright's 'genius':

'Certainly, if Wright's plan appears to be "queer," his business methods are more so. Probably his loose methods are a mere indication of his great genius – because if a man is a genius, he must be a little off in other respects …'

And so, while trying to persuade his architect to be more reliable, more punctual and more consistent in his plans and budgets, he ended up accepting the treatment he got from Wright, believing that he was gaining the inestimable benefit of employing a genius. He and his wife ended up moving in, in 1905, with the house not quite complete. To the end, they were forced to compromise while Wright pursued his vision.

Vision and reality

The problems would have been easier to bear if the couple had both liked their house. While Darwin Martin was impressed, and seemed unable, for all his complaints about the cost, to say a firm 'no' to Wright when he suggested alterations or upgrades, his wife was less than enthusiastic. She didn't like her bedroom, and failed to persuade Wright to alter it to her specifications. And she felt that the main living room was too dark – mainly because of the size of the shady covered porch that led off it. In later life, when she began to lose her eyesight, she felt this lack of light still more deeply.

ABOVE The living and dining rooms are large adjacent spaces open to one another and benefiting from natural light through big windows facing north and east. The eastern windows (those on the right in the picture) are French windows that open on to a veranda that is as big as the living room itself.

Plan of first floor

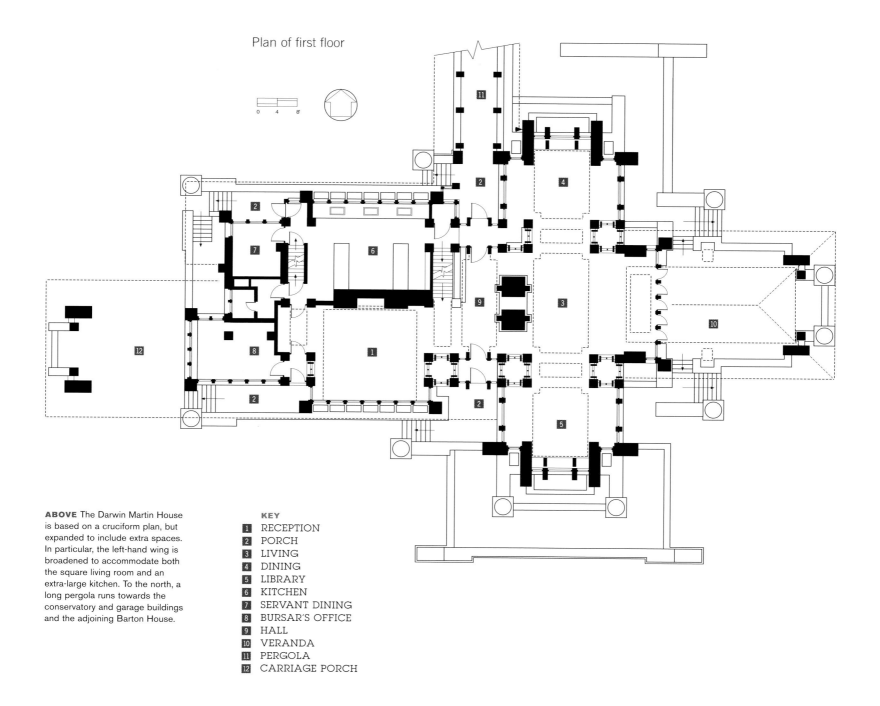

0 4 8'

ABOVE The Darwin Martin House is based on a cruciform plan, but expanded to include extra spaces. In particular, the left-hand wing is broadened to accommodate both the square living room and an extra-large kitchen. To the north, a long pergola runs towards the conservatory and garage buildings and the adjoining Barton House.

KEY

1 RECEPTION
2 PORCH
3 LIVING
4 DINING
5 LIBRARY
6 KITCHEN
7 SERVANT DINING
8 BURSAR'S OFFICE
9 HALL
10 VERANDA
11 PERGOLA
12 CARRIAGE PORCH

For all its faults, though, the house represents an impressive vision, the ultimate Prairie House merging with its large garden and standing out between tall trees. Inside, too, the interlocking living spaces are generous, and the rhythms Wright created of grouped brick columns, ceiling beams, rectangular windows and curvaceous fireplaces are on the grand scale. Impressive too is the way Wright was able to define interior spaces without conventional walls – the divisions between the rooms are created by the piers, screens, beams and built-in furniture. This is the fluid interior par excellence.

And yet to some visitors, at least, there's something cold and grandiose – and not a little dark – about this self-consciously 'great' interior. And the exterior, which Wright so carefully integrated into the garden, sustained major damage when the long pergola and garage block were demolished, leaving the house cut loose from its moorings. The house cannot quite bear all the weight of greatness that architect and client so badly wanted.

In recent years, however, the building's fortunes have improved. In the 1990s a corporation was formed to restore the house. Some intrusive later apartment buildings have been removed from the site and the demolished Wright structures have been rebuilt. The house itself is now looking as good as ever as the result of the restoration project.

Barton House

On one corner of the large plot occupied by the Darwin Martin House sits another Wright building, the house he built for Mrs Martin's sister, Delta, and her husband, George Barton. The Barton House is like a tiny version of the Darwin Martin residence. It has the same brick walls as the larger building, and similar overhanging pitched roofs. There is no mistaking, though, that this modest house, tucked away in a corner of the site, is the 'poor relation' of the two, although some visitors prefer it to its grander neighbour.

Location
Buffalo, New York

Client
Darwin D. Martin,
George Barton and
Delta Martin Barton

Date
1903

Main materials
Brick

The house was born of idealism. Darwin Martin and his brother, William, had had a hard childhood and youth. They left home early to become door-to-door salesmen, selling soap for the Larkin Company. Their American dream came true and both rose to become successful in business. But Darwin Martin always regretted the way his family broke up, and vowed, in building his house, to do what he could to bring it back together again. Hence the house for his sister and her husband George, who worked for the Larkin Company, on the same plot as his own residence.

Design and budget This is a much smaller house than the Darwin Martin residence – its footprint is not that much bigger than the Darwin Martin garage building – and it is very much a subsidiary structure. Some authorities on Wright have claimed that the architect spent little time on its design.

The floor plan, after all, was based on an earlier Wright house, the one he designed for J.J. Walser in Chicago in 1902. Even so, it went over budget just as predictably as the main house, and Darwin Martin complained, but dug into his wallet, when he realised that the finished building would cost him more than $9,000.

Although the Barton House is small, Wright's design makes it feel bigger than it is. The way he merges the interior living areas – the living, dining and reception spaces – helps make the house feel more spacious. Upstairs, where privacy is more important, the two main bedrooms are positioned at either end of a corridor.

Patterns of glass
As with many of Wright's earlier houses, the architect employed intricately patterned coloured glass in the windows. In contrast to his larger houses, though, where there are often many different 'art-glass' designs, Wright repeated a single pattern throughout all the decorated windows in the Barton House. Although Wright's work on the main Darwin Martin House was hardly budget-conscious, he no doubt felt that this approach was more appropriate to the 'lesser' house on the site, while giving it most of the advantages – a varied surface texture and reflectivity, a feeling of richness, interesting shadows and colours in the interior, and so on – provided by this kind of glazing.

The compact Barton House was the first of the buildings to be completed on the Buffalo site. In some ways it was a rehearsal for the main house, in the sense that it allowed Darwin Martin and Wright to test the waters of their relationship and see how they would get on as architect and client. This is an unusual luxury – most people commission only one building – and in some ways it did little to prevent the tensions that erupted when Wright began work in earnest on the big house. But the period of construction enabled Wright and Martin to develop a friendship, and this saw them through the lengthy construction period of the main house, which was not signed off by Wright until 1907, two years after the Martins had moved in.

House and context
The siting of the Barton House in one corner of the Martin plot indicated its subsidiary status. But Wright's design of the main house, with its long pergola linking it to the conservatory and carriage house, actually helped to link the Barton House visually to its larger sibling, symbolizing the family unity that was so important to Darwin Martin. This architectural link was destroyed in the 1960s when the then owner of the big house demolished the pergola and carriage house and sold off the land on which they stood for development. This effectively isolated the Barton House; but now work is

LEFT The Barton House stands like a small pavilion near the Darwin Martin residence and, next to the huge house, could be mistaken for a servant's cottage or a guest house. Wright related the building to its larger sibling with the use of similar brickwork and broad, overhanging roofs.

RIGHT Art glass and fine woodwork enhance the interior of the house, giving the building some of the quality that the architect lavished on its larger neighbour. Wright was often keen to point out that smaller houses should be designed with as much care as grander ones on big budgets.

advanced on restoring the whole complex. The pergola and conservatory have been rebuilt (this is the first rebuilding of a major demolished structure by Wright), and the George Barton House can once more be seen in proper relation to the Martins' residence.

The two houses can also now be seen together as two different aspects of Wright's architecture. The two buildings share a palette of pale brick, shallow hipped roofs and bands of windows outside, of oak and art glass within. They also share a similar design approach with the small gardener's cottage on the complex, which is also being restored. But their differences – the one grand, the other intimate – are also revealed. They have become part of a complex devoted to the preservation and study of Wright's work, where visitors can learn at first hand how this American genius went about designing and bringing to reality the houses for which he is so famous.

Hardy House

The house that Wright designed for Thomas P. Hardy, then mayor of Racine, Wisconsin, shows a daring use of a difficult site. Perched on a slope above Lake Michigan, the house exploits the drama of the location with its striking mix of horizontal rooflines and strong uprights. The building is a good example of how an apparently uninviting site could inspire Wright to rise to the challenge of designing quite a modest house in a memorable way.

Location
Racine, Wisconsin
Client
Thomas P. Hardy
Date
1905
Main materials
Wood, plaster

RIGHT The small windows on the street frontage are glazed with art glass. Here the patterns fill up quite a large area of the window, because protecting the owners' privacy was more important than allowing them to look out at the street. The mainly clear glass still lets plenty of light into the interior.

The site posed special challenges but also offered unique rewards. The plot slopes quite steeply away from the road, but at the back commands views of Lake Michigan. To make best use of the flatter land near the road, Wright placed the house very close to the sidewalk — he often liked to build close to the road, but this house is closer than most. Most of the larger windows on this side are on the upper floors, to give the occupants some privacy, but on the other side there are more windows and a balcony, to give views of the lake. In this way the building's two 'faces' — one suburban, one oriented towards the lake scenery — work well.

A symmetrical layout Unusually for Wright, the house is very symmetrical. It is flanked by matching Japanese-style enclosed gardens and there are even two front doors. Wright seemed to enjoy the tension between the very ordered layout and the natural scenery that the house overlooks.

The plan is very compact. Wright did not use his favourite cruciform configuration for the Hardy House. Instead he devised a plan made up of three overlapping squares — a large square in the centre and two smaller ones arranged symmetrically on either side. This pattern of squares is hinted at in the pattern of the leaded glass in the entrance hall windows, as if Wright were leaving behind a clue to his special thinking. The architect often mirrored aspects of his planning in decorative details like this — it was one of his ways of achieving an integrated or holistic design.

One further element in the plan is the large balcony that opens off the main downstairs room, giving views on to the lake. This is an open balcony, so, unlike the covered porch of the Darwin Martin House (see page 55), it does not block light from the house. From the garden, though, it looks massive, because it has a tall retaining wall, made necessary by the sloping site of the house.

The influence of Japan

The Japanese influence is made very clear in a drawing of the house by Wright's associate Marion Mahony, in which the building is seen from below the balcony and framed by the outlines of the surrounding trees and shrubs. The house is portrayed in relation to its environment, and the style of the drawing, with its stylized trees and creative use of white space, owes a lot to the Japanese prints that Wright loved. There is something Japanese too in the strong vertical lines of the house – the window uprights of the lakeside elevation and the vertical timbers of the street frontage, which stand out against the white walls. The architectural writer and scholar Vincent Scully Jr, in his book about the architect, wrote that the house was 'rendered by Wright as an incident in a Japanese screen'. Others have seen both the 'timber-framed' effect of the walls and the use of leaded glass in the windows as drawing on the Japanese influence.

The drawing, no less than the house itself, shows how Wright liked to create drama from his architecture. There is something playful about the way the building clings to its bluff above the lake and something defiant about the way the house stands out from its more conventional neighbours on the street. The locals could not fail to notice this, of course, and most of them were amused by the strange-looking building that had risen in their midst. Some took to laughing at it, maybe sensing something alien and un-American in this odd cuckoo in its Midwestern nest. Perhaps this was why Wright built little in this city in his native state until, more than two decades later, he began work on his buildings for Johnson Wax (see pages 112–115).

As usual with Wright, the details in the house are as interesting and meticulous as the planning and massing. One example of this care over detail is the windows. Like many Wright houses, the Thomas Hardy House has windows containing the art glass that the architect was so fond of. Narrow strips of coloured glass, made of patterns of rectangles and squares held together with 'leading' that is actually made of zinc, are arranged around the edges of each opening. They make an elegant 'frame within the window frame'. The owners of the Racine property have looked after these windows with care – something of a challenge because the house is sited so close to the sidewalk and some years ago vandals began to smash some of the glass. The owners responded with a pragmatic solution – covering the glazing in protective clear plastic sheeting. This reduces the glittering effect of the art glass from outside, but has done a good job of protecting the precious material.

Robie House

Robie House

The Robie House is the ultimate Prairie House. Its finely crafted 'Roman' brick walls and perfectly balanced cantilevered roofs are as stunning and well composed as an abstract painting by Mondrian. The overhanging roofs are also artful in another way, shading the house at midday, but letting in plenty of light when and where it is needed. The house is a masterpiece of both style and substance.

Location
Chicago, Illinois

Client
Frederick C. Robie

Date
1906

Main materials
Brick, steel

'I know what you want – one of those damn Wright houses.' Frederick C. Robie was an inventor and manufacturer – of automobile and bicycle parts – who had 'made it'. A practical man who knew what he wanted, he jotted down his ideas for the kind of house he needed for himself, his wife and their young family. When he showed his ideas to builders, that brusque response was the one that stuck in his mind. So he went to see Wright, and they got on.

A modern house Robie wanted a modern house, which for him meant two things: first, it would be a clutter-free dwelling in a modern architectural idiom; second, it would be full of the latest technology. The builders who Robie consulted knew that Frank Lloyd Wright was the man who could deliver on these requirements. And so it proved. Wright was at his most creative when responding to Robie's requests, designing perhaps the greatest of all his Prairie Houses.

Space and place Spatially the house is remarkable. The Wright hallmarks are refined and expanded to striking effect. Long roofs are cantilevered far out over the porches and balconies, hovering above them with little visible means of support, and providing shelter and protection from glare. Large living rooms are glazed with the architect's usual lavishness, opening the house to the garden. The main living room is on the upper floor – set above the children's playroom and the billiard room – so benefiting from good views and plenty of light.

The house is artfully positioned on its lot. The local standard was to set back the buildings some 35 feet (11 m) from the sidewalk. This went against the instincts of Wright, who liked to build as near to the street as he could, as if his houses were reaching out to embrace arriving visitors. He solved the dilemma by respecting the building line with the main walls, but throwing out both his cantilevered roofs and the garden wall beyond it, so that the house seemed to extend right up to the sidewalk. Naturally, the garden wall is built of the same 'Roman' brick – topped and tailed with pale masonry, as the rest of the house – so that it 'reads' as part of the structure.

Structure and technology As this structure went up, onlookers watched in amazement. Although from the outside the house looks like a brick building, the structural heart of it is the steelwork: long beams that support the magically cantilevered roofs.

LEFT In strong sunlight, the Robie House shows its impressive design to best advantage, with its brick walls bathed in light and the huge overhanging roofs in contrasting shadow. The long row of windows lets in plenty of natural light to the living and dining rooms, while the porches provide shade, giving Frederick C. Robie the best of both worlds.

RIGHT A view from the front deck shows the fine brickwork, its horizontal mortar courses clearly emphasized, that makes up the walls of the Robie House. Planters are integrated into the stone coping at some points, to bring nature close to this suburban house.

KEY
1 PORCH
2 LIVING
3 DINING
4 BALCONY
5 GUEST
6 BATH
7 KITCHEN
8 SERVANT'S DINING
9 SERVANT
10 CORRIDOR
11 FIRE

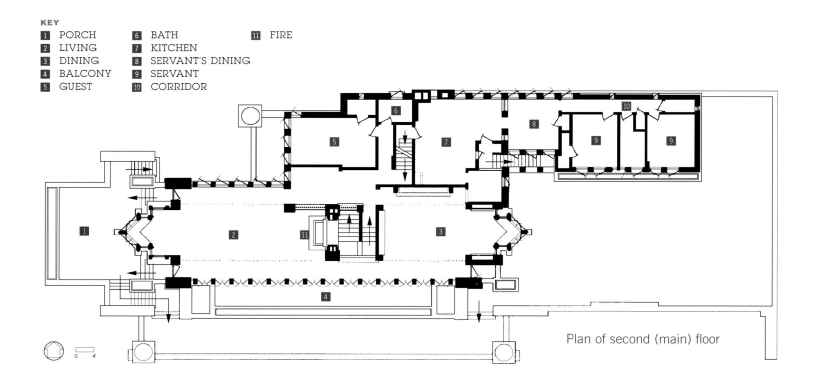

Plan of second (main) floor

Even those who passed the site regularly, watching as the beams were bolted together, were impressed by the sheer length of the cantilevers, made possible by the structure. With its long lines and vast 'decks', it was one of those houses that make people think of an ocean liner. It, and Wright, were clearly going places.

If the planning is everything we have come to expect of Wright, the technology was even more so. The house benefited from the best and latest in electric lighting (with fittings designed by Wright), burglar and fire alarms, the most up-to-date telephones and an industrial-type vacuum-cleaning system. Robie the inventor was satisfied, as he no doubt was by the commodious triple garage for his automobiles.

It all cost a lot, even if, at around $60,000, it was a fraction of the price of the Darwin Martin House. But there were no disagreements between client and architect about the budget this time. Robie knew he was creating something special, and had confidence in Wright's ability to produce it. Perhaps it was because both men, in their different ways, were innovators and engineers and could admire one another's skill. Both knew too that this kind of innovation rarely comes cheap.

The clients and their house

By all accounts, the Robies were happy with their house. If Frederick liked the technology and the space, his wife responded positively to the lightness, the garden, and the space provided for the children. But they were not destined to live long in their architectural masterpiece. Within two years of moving in, the couple were divorced, Robie having cheated on his wife. The house was sold.

Robie's troubles did not end there. Soon his father died, leaving vast debts, which the son – a man of honour in his financial dealings, at least – felt he should pay off. The cost of this wiped out Robie's fortune and he never recovered financially. The house survived, however, even though it lost some of its features, such as the wall that screened off the garage court. Much of the furniture that Wright designed specially for the house has gone too, depriving the interiors of the coherence they once had. On its Chicago street, surrounded by other buildings, it does rather look like a Prairie House that has travelled a long way from its natural home. But it is still one of Wright's greatest buildings, a testimony to what can happen when architect and client share a clear and radical vision.

ABOVE The plan of the main floor of the Robie House is surprisingly simple. The two main living rooms with the stairs between them make up one long rectangle. An adjoining rectangle of a similar size houses the service accommodation and a guest room. Beyond these blocks, the balcony and porch that give the house its striking character extend to the south and west.

OPPOSITE TOP The main part of the dining room is reserved for a large table with high-backed chairs, but beyond there is a more intimate space, an inglenook with a pointed bay window. It was important in a large house to provide smaller, more private spaces as well as large rooms for entertaining.

OPPOSITE BOTTOM The living room is one of Wright's lightest. The French windows on the left open on to the balcony overlooking the street. The windows in the centre lead to the large, shady porch. There are yet more windows out of shot to the right. At night, two long rows of spherical lamps flood the room with light.

LEFT The art glass in the Robie House windows is both intricate and beautiful. The patterns are made up of a complex mixture of diamonds, triangles, parallelograms and other shapes. Wright liked to integrate the decoration into his designs in this way, scorning such decorative add-ons as wallpaper.

Coonley House

Set in its estate in Riverside, Illinois, the Coonley House is a vast building, sprawling among gardens, courtyards and trees. The large complex, including a gardener's cottage and stables (now converted to a separate dwelling), is unified visually by the use of pale walls, dark window frames and shallow pitched roofs. The interiors are impressive, too: dominated by their many windows and skylights and big, pitched, timber-framed ceilings, giving a generous sense of height and space.

Location
Riverside, Illinois

Client
Avery Coonley and
Queene Ferry Coonley

Date
1907

Main materials
Brick, glass

Avery Coonley was a graduate of Harvard and MIT who worked in his family's business for a few years before devoting himself to his philanthropic interests, to his passion for education and to Christian Science. His wife, Queene, a member of the rich Ferry family, had studied education and shared her husband's interests. The couple were also devoted to the arts and entertained on a lavish and formal scale.

The importance of 'principle'

When the Coonleys decided to build themselves a house, they took time to look at many recent houses, including a number designed by Wright – they probably went to an exhibition including his work in the Art Institute of Chicago. Wright's work attracted them strongly, Mrs Coonley saying that they found in it 'the countenances of principle'. As Christian Scientists the Coonleys believed that if something were based on sound principles then its execution would be sound too. This was therefore a compliment and Wright was understandably pleased. He resolved to do his best for the Coonleys and they put their considerable fortune at his disposal.

The house that Wright built for Coonley was one of his largest. Unlike many of the Prairie Houses, it is a courtyard building in which the living accommodation and service buildings are arranged in a U-shape around a central garden area. The house is 'zoned' – in other words, different parts of the 'U' contain rooms of different functions: living rooms in one section, service rooms in another, bedrooms and guest rooms in the third. Unlike the traditional courtyard house, the principal rooms have their main outlook not over the courtyard but over the surrounding grounds, into which the rambling house sprawls. The low-slung design is enhanced with typical Wright touches such as leaded-glass windows, specially designed lamps and – a new departure for Wright – polychrome tiles. So the Coonley House is an outward-looking building that marries the courtyard and Prairie House principles. This is a successful marriage, and Wright was proud of the house, rating it his favourite when he wrote his autobiography – although at that point many of his greatest houses, such as Fallingwater, had yet to be built.

Interior spaces

The Coonley House is a grand house for a rich client, but it does not have a grand entrance. The door is hidden away in a rather shadowy spot under a porch. This is not unusual with Wright: he is not often an architect of showy doorways. He was more interested in what happened as you entered the building, in the process of discovering the house. So at the Coonley House, the visitor enters in the shadows and walks up three steps to a landing. From here a stairway goes up to the next floor, where the main reception rooms are located. Ascending the stair, you walk into the

OPPOSITE This façade of the large Coonley House looks modest – the pale range of buildings does not look as if it is part of a big house. With his keen sense of the theatrical, Wright sometimes liked to surprise visitors to his houses, building a simple frontage or small entry that leads to much larger and more impressive spaces.

RIGHT The Coonley living room has a much more impressive exterior, on which several elements – such as the uprights between the windows and the ironwork – are richly patterned. In the foreground is one of the planters that Wright used on many of his houses, a round bowl set in a square surround.

LEFT Wright provided the
sprawling Coonley House with lots
of windows looking out over the
grounds in all directions. Windows
to the east of the bedroom wing
admit the morning sun, while
glazing facing east, west and north
illuminates the main living rooms
during the day, looking out over
the planting that Wright marked
on the plan.

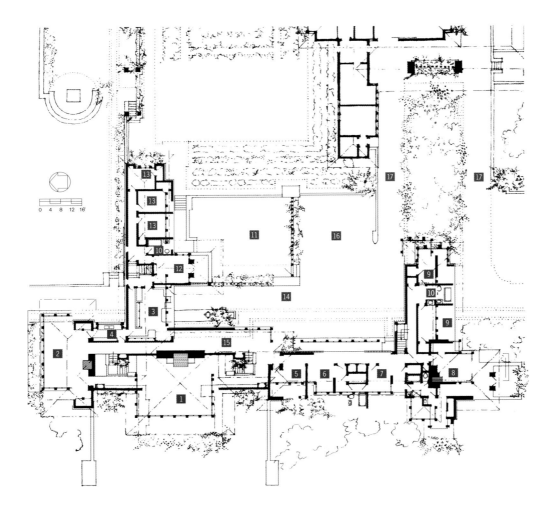

Main floor plan

KEY

1 LIVING
2 DINING
3 KITCHEN
4 PANTRY
5 STUDY
6 BED
7 CHILDREN'S BED
8 PARENTS' BED
9 GUEST BED
10 BATH
11 SERVANT'S COURT
12 SERVANT
13 MAID
14 DRIVE
15 HALL
16 COURT
17 INCLINED DRIVE

light, for, in contrast to the rather dark lower floor, the main rooms are beautifully lit. So you are drawn along, first towards the dining room (lit by windows on three sides), then down a skylit gallery to the living room, another light and imposing space. Again, this room is lit by windows on three sides. The fourth side houses the fireplace, with its long mural of forest scenery – fern and birch designs in autumnal colours – on either side, so that there is a sense of the landscape enveloping the room, both in the form of the real scenery glimpsed through the windows and of the trees in the mural.

Because these main rooms are on the upper floor of the house, the first floor is little more than a basement and the playroom is the only important room on this lower floor. The living rooms therefore command good views over the garden. Wright filled these living rooms with specially designed furniture. Even the carpet on the living room-floor was made especially to the architect's design, and he made sure that the pattern in the carpet, which was handmade in Austria, reflected the designs of other details in the house.

The later history of the house
The Coonleys lived in their house until they moved to Washington DC in 1917, when Avery Coonley was invited to do public relations and lobbying work for the Church of Christ Scientist in the District of Columbia. He died in Washington in 1920, but his wife lived for another 38 years, and did not forget Wright. When the architect, like so many other Americans, fell on hard times in the late 1920s, she was one of the group of clients who rallied round, paid off his debts and saved him financially.

In the 1950s an architect and developer called Arnold Skrow bought the property and split it up, making two separate homes out of the huge house and turning the stable and gardener's cottage into separate dwellings too. It was a compromise, but one that allowed Wright's great house to survive. Although still subdivided, it is now in the hands of caring owners.

Meyer May House

A compact building in tan brick with pitched red-tiled roofs, the Meyer May House is an example of the way Frank Lloyd Wright could create a near-perfect design with limited means. The small details – such as the copper roof-trim, the art-glass windows, and the specially made furniture – make this an outstanding example of the small Prairie House.

Location
Grand Rapids, Michigan

Client
Meyer May

Date
1908

Main materials
Brick, glass

Businessman Meyer May, who had made his money in the clothing business, came to Wright in 1908 for a house for himself, his wife Sophie and their two adopted children. For many, the house Wright produced was one of his best. It is not a large building, but in its design the architect managed to marry his aesthetic flair with a practical approach that made the place comfortable and good to live in. Thanks to a particularly happy restoration in 1987–8, it is once more a perfect Wright house, a beautifully crafted example of Wright's special blend of traditional and modern, standing out like an architectural beacon among the more conventional houses in the neighbourhood.

Tricks of design The exterior is dominated by sweeping cantilevered roofs. Some of these roofs overhang so much that it seems amazing that they do not fall down under the weight of Michigan's winter snows. Wright was sailing close to the wind here and risking structural damage or collapse, an

issue that was finally resolved when the house was restored in the 1980s. There is no faulting the detailing, though. Copper trim lines the roofs and its colour is picked up in the window frames, giving the outside a feeling of harmony. For the brickwork, Wright used his trick of emphasizing the horizontal mortar joints by raking them out and using darker mortar. The effect is to draw subtle horizontal lines around the building, something that the casual visitor hardly notices, but which helps suggest subliminally that the building is low and horizontal.

Entering the house entails experiencing another typical Wright trick — the hidden, dark entryway that leads into main living rooms flooded with light. The first of these rooms is the dining room, which is dominated by the Wright-designed dining table. At its corners stand four large light standards, each with a stained-glass shade on top of a tall wooden pedestal. They spread warm light over the table and make a very effective statement from wherever you sit or stand. This is not a large room, but the layout and furnishing make it imposing — no doubt the Mays' friends were impressed when they sat down for a meal.

Decorative effects
The other main space, the living room, is focused on the fireplace. Here Wright emphasized the horizontal mortar courses not with darker mortar but with an inlay of brightly shining glass or tile. This catches the light — during the day from the numerous windows and skylights, and at night from the fire itself — and makes the fireplace shimmer. A simple effect, it gives the room a memorable richness of texture, which is enhanced by the art glass in the windows and by the strong patterning in the window glazing bars.

Further decorative effects come from the work of Milwaukee interior specialist George Niedecken, who collaborated with Wright on many of his houses, creating furniture and murals to the architect's specifications. A delightful hollyhock mural by Niedecken is a notable feature in the Meyer May House.

Upstairs, the bedrooms are simpler. Wright pragmatically held that rich decoration was not so important in rooms in which people spent most of their time asleep. So, with the exception of some more glittering glass inserted in the mortar around the fireplace in the master bedroom, simple finishes are the order of the day. The rich woods of furniture, floors and other fittings provide all the colour that is needed. The sloping ceilings provide added spatial interest.

Restoration
For some time, though, Wright's unified vision for this fine house was compromised. Over the years the house was extended, and by the 1980s it was looking the worse for wear and a far cry from the structure Wright designed. Fortunately for Wright's legacy, however, the building was purchased

LEFT The Meyer May House is one of those in which there is only minimal masonry on the upper floor, which is lit by strips of windows. The resulting lack of upper walls makes the roof seem to float above the house. This view shows the terrace, with the living and dining rooms behind. The entrance is hidden away at the other side of the house.

RIGHT The details on this Prairie House are particularly carefully worked, as this photograph of the living room French windows shows. Wright seems to have relished the combination of copper cladding and light brown brickwork, designing more complex window openings than usual, the rectangles reflecting the smaller patterns in the art glass.

by Steelcase Inc., the office furniture company that produced the furnishings for Wright's Johnson Wax buildings (see pages 112–115). Steelcase set about restoring the house. Aiming to bring the building back to the way it looked when it was new, the restorers demolished the extension. Setting to work on Wright's vision, they researched the architect's original plans and drawings, and compared them with his other designs and extant buildings. Gradually the house was repaired, and one structural issue — the daring cantilevered roof — was addressed with the insertion of more supportive steelwork. Now the weight of the roof, and the winter snow load, are supported as never before.

The original decorations were restored, and the house was furnished with a mixture of original pieces, reproduction Wright furniture and compatible items in the Arts and Crafts style from around the time it was built. The house is now open to the public so that visitors and students can appreciate the architect's achievement. The restored building is a powerful tribute to the master's capacity for taking pains.

Coonley Playhouse

This small building is in the grounds of the house that Frank Lloyd Wright
built for Avery and Queene Coonley in Riverside, Illinois. An elegant structure
on a cross-shaped plan with pale walls and flat roofs, it is an impressive exercise
in solid forms and planes, a design that is more important and impressive than
its small size suggests. An unusual project for Wright, it was built as a small
school, but has subsequently been converted for residential use.

Location
Riverside, Illinois

Client
Queene Ferry Coonley

Date
1911

Main materials
Concrete, glass

Avery Coonley and his wife Queene Ferry Coonley were among Wright's richest clients. When they had settled in the large house in Riverside, Illinois that Wright designed for them (see pages 64–67), they began to plan a new building, reflecting their interest in education.

School and stage
As Christian Scientists, the Coonleys had strong beliefs about education and the bringing up of their daughter. Avery Coonley was also a director of *The Dial*, a political and literary magazine that was published in Chicago but gained a national reputation for its discussions of books, writers, and trends in politics. But the Coonleys' involvement was also on a more practical level than this. Queene Coonley was an experienced and qualified teacher and started a small 'cottage school' for her daughter and a number of other children in the neighbourhood. They commissioned Wright to design a school building near their Riverside house.

Because it has a stage and has been used for theatrical performances, the structure is now known as the Coonley Playhouse. It is a pale-walled building, its predominantly light colour relieved at the front by three strong vertical bands of glazing. There are flat roofs, which overhang in several directions, providing shade, and trees and shrubs have grown up around the walls, softening its lines and making it rise from the garden more organically than it must have done when it first appeared, new and white, in 1911–12.

OPPOSITE Outside, the trio of big windows, the overhanging roofs and the large central block with its smaller flanking wings set up a satisfying composition of shapes and forms. This highly linear building is saved from looking stark by the way it blends in with the surrounding trees.

RIGHT The glass in the Playhouse windows is rather different from Wright's usual art glass – the balloon-like circles and primary colours seem just right for a building used by children. The design has proved very popular and is now licensed for use on all kinds of objects, from lamps to wall clocks.

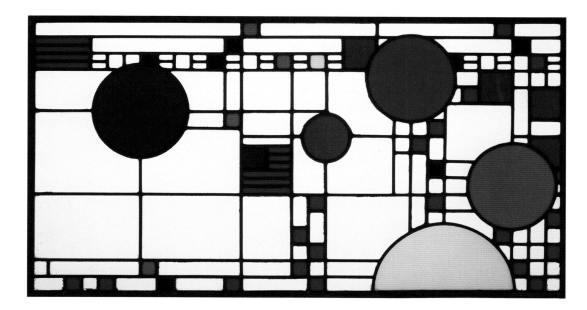

This is a small building but many have admired its flair and elegance, and books and articles about Wright have given it more prominence than one might guess from its small size. Henry-Russell Hitchcock, in his pioneering 1942 book on Wright, refers to the 'virtuosity of poised planes and balanced masses' demonstrated on the building's exterior, while finding the interior rather heavier and more 'architectural'. He rightly finds similarities between this building and the pavilions of Wright's large Midway Gardens scheme – both, in their different ways, were buildings connected with culture and entertainment. Hitchcock also admires the way in which Wright tried to create an identity of scale inside and outside the building.

The Playhouse is not a theatre in the conventional meaning of the term, but because the Coonleys were interested in the theatre, and believed that it should be an element in their child's education, the interior of the school was built with a raised area at one end, which could be used as a stage.

Balloons and confetti windows
The Coonley Playhouse is a cruciform building lit by tall windows at one end and high, clerestory windows on either side. Its main space is the school assembly room. Wright decorated its windows with charming art-glass designs in strong primary colours, using a motif known as 'balloons and confetti'. This design may have been inspired by a similar one in the floor of the Petit Palais in Paris, which Wright would probably have seen when he visited the French capital in 1910. Although the Playhouse is now a residence, some of these windows can still be seen in New York's Museum of Modern Art; others are now privately owned. The windows have also provided the inspiration for various commercially available objects, including jewellery, cups and plates.

Reproductions of the original clerestory windows were made and fitted during the late 1980s. These have been made of white glass with a very thin layer of colour applied to the surface. William Allin Storrer, in *The Architecture of Frank Lloyd Wright: A Complete Catalog*, has explained the significance of this technique and the difference from conventional stained glass: 'This allows the glass to appear plain outside during the day, yet the design inside is brightly colored; stained glass would be visible outside and would not be as bright inside. At night, the pattern is visible outside, but appears as pastel color; with stained glass, the color would be bright outside at night.' This beautiful glass helped turn a rather severe pale box of a building into something richer – a schoolroom that must have been both appealing and stimulating to the children who learned and played there.

Taliesin

Taliesin has become synonymous with Frank Lloyd Wright. Planned as both the architect's home and the base of his architectural practice, it combined these different functions elegantly. But successive fires destroyed parts of the building and would have destroyed the life of a man less determined to carry on than Wright. The architect doggedly rebuilt his home, and much of what survives today is from the 1925 rebuild.

Location
Spring Green, Wisconsin
Client
The architect
Date
1911, 1925
Main materials
Stone, wood, glass

The years 1909 to 1911 saw a crisis in Wright's life. He left his wife Catherine for Mamah Borthwick Cheney, the wife of his Oak Park neighbour and client Edwin Cheney, and eventually left the USA with Mamah Cheney for a year-long stay in Europe. Finding his various assistants unwilling to take over his architectural practice in his absence, Wright left it in the hands of a little-known German architect called Hermann von Holst. When he returned to America in 1911, Wright was faced with the task of rebuilding his Chicago practice. He also decided to build a country house and workplace for himself on land belonging to his mother's family at Spring Green, Wisconsin.

House and hillside Wright called his new house Taliesin, the name of an ancient, possibly mythical British poet. Literally the word means 'shining brow', and no doubt Wright chose it because he built the house on a hillside. The architect himself, though, did not hold with the idea of building a house *on* a hill: '… no house should ever be put *on* a hill or *on* anything. It should be *of* the hill. Belonging to it. Hill and house should live together each the happier for the other.' In the 'organic' architecture that Wright championed, house and landscape should be as one.

The house was planned in a rather similar way to Wright's house for Avery Coonley, although on a much less grand scale. Like the Coonley House, Taliesin had a courtyard and the buildings were arranged around it in a U-shape. At each end was a large wing: one containing the main house, the other a service area with stables, garages and a cowshed. Connecting these two wings was a narrow building containing a long workroom and a loggia. This loggia was a key feature because it was the way through which you entered the house and it provided a stunning view over the valley before you turned into the entrance hall.

The building was to be one that Wright continuously modified and rebuilt. But although there were many changes and expansions, natural materials – stone walls, cedar shingles, woollen rugs – were always predominant and gave a sense of continuity. Many of the stone walls are left unplastered inside the house, heightening the sense of unity between interior and exterior. And this unity is further enhanced by the use of stone in the garden. From the living room, you look out past stone interior walls to stone outer walls, and towards garden walls and paths also made of stone.

From the beginning, this house, grounded in the Wisconsin countryside, meant many things to Wright. It was planned as a home and workplace away from the city – a place where he could live in tranquillity

RIGHT Beautifully set at the top of a slope, Taliesin is designed to provide its occupants with good views – but also to dominate the hillside where it sits. Yet this building, for all its size and dominance, does not seem imposed on the slope but appears to emerge from it, its outline broken up and softened by the surrounding trees.

with Mamah Cheney, somewhere from which he could draw inspiration from a landscape of rare beauty, a base for his group of apprentices, and also a place where he could connect with his mother's Wisconsin ancestry.

A media firestorm

Wright and Cheney did not achieve their hoped-for tranquillity, however. They created a furore, and Wright himself, while claiming he wanted to be left in peace, fanned the flames of a media fire. The couple moved to Taliesin in 1911, and Wright – getting wind of public disapproval of his relationship with Cheney – called a defiant press conference on Christmas Day to justify his conduct.

It was an extraordinary and badly timed action, and when the press arrived the architect read out a self-justifying statement attempting to explain his actions. He asked the reporters to give him a chance, to 'go slow in deciding that he [had] acted badly'; but the newspapers showed no mercy, denouncing Wright for deserting his children on Christmas Day, of all days.

Instead of letting the fire die down, Wright retaliated and issued a written statement, couched in somewhat pompous prose, offering further justifications. He claimed that his first marriage had been the mistake of a young man, that he loved Mamah, that he had had a genuine struggle with his conscience, but that in the end he could only 'carry out life's purpose' with Mamah at his side. In spite of his best efforts, he said, 'the hue and cry of the yellow press was raised, the man and woman defamed'.

Needless to say, the representatives of the 'yellow press' did not take kindly to this description, and the pointless public bickering continued for some days. Eventually, Wright returned to his work, absorbing himself in the commissions that were beginning to come in again, and continuing his emotional commitment to Mamah and to his new house, Taliesin.

Disaster and recovery

But if the architect made a huge emotional investment in the place, this was to be put under the severest strain. In August 1914, when Wright was working in Chicago, a deranged servant armed with a hatchet went on a murderous rampage through the house, killing seven people before setting the place on fire. Much of the residential part of the building was destroyed, only the stone parts surviving the flames. The working part of the house escaped largely unscathed. The dead were William Weston, a favourite carpenter who worked with Wright; an apprentice, Emil Brodelle; workers David Lindblom and Thomas Brunker; and Mamah Cheney and her two children.

Wright was devastated. He had spent five years rebuilding his emotional life, and now everything he had worked for was gone. To add to his pain, he had to cope with the moralizing criticisms of many commentators, who argued that what had happened was just punishment for an adulterous couple. But Wright's Spring Green neighbours were more supportive, and the tragedy seemed to increase Wright's determination to make something of the place. He quickly set about rebuilding the house, very much to the original plan.

But this was not the end of the story. In 1925 the house caught fire again, this time as the result of a lightning strike. In the same year, Wright once more began a rebuild, taking the opportunity to make the house larger. The drafting room filled up with apprentices, and life went on in the extended house. With the workroom so crowded, Wright himself usually worked in a small private room, where he had a view of the courtyard and the peace to work on his drawings. In spaces dominated by natural materials such as stone and wood, and looking out over a landscape of Wisconsin countryside and artificial lakes that Wright had dug in the ground, the architect could continue to produce designs for buildings that were 'of' their surroundings and grounded in the American landscape.

FRANK LLOYD WRIGHT spent the years 1916 to 1922 working on the Imperial Hotel, Tokyo, staying in Japan most of the time. His practice in the USA continued, with Wright making trips back to advise and check on progress. Although he had relatively few American projects at this time, he did complete two major houses, one for Frederick Bogk in Milwaukee, Wisconsin, and the much larger Hollyhock House in Los Angeles. The success of Hollyhock House was no doubt one factor that encouraged Wright to set up a new office in California after he had completed his work in Tokyo in 1922. He believed that he could give California a better kind of domestic architecture, different from the pseudo-Spanish designs that were popular there, and began to design in a style very different from his earlier Prairie Houses.

Wright's new departure was to build houses using concrete blocks. This was a very unusual thing to do – concrete was still a material that people looked down on, and if it was used in building it was often hidden under some more 'attractive' material such as stone or brick. But Wright devised a kind of cast concrete block that could be made on site by unskilled labour, that was light enough for one person to lift easily, that could be laid with ease, and that looked good too.

For Wright, the added attraction of the concrete block was that you could cast decoration into it, and Wright's California concrete-block houses are covered with relief decoration that catches the strong sunlight and gives these buildings a unique texture. The architect produced just four memorable houses using this method. Although this did not represent enough work to turn his practice around, these are four of his best-loved buildings, in which the unlikely material blends well with dramatic hilly sites and lush trees and garden plants. Against the odds, houses and settings combine wonderfully.

SET IN CONCRETE

Bogk House

A perfectly symmetrical façade facing the street gives the Bogk House a formality quite unlike most Wright houses of this period. The enormous overhanging roof, however, together with the row of slightly projecting windows, makes this unmistakeably one of Wright's designs. Its layout owes a lot to the formal pavilions of the architect's Imperial Hotel, but the treatment is more restrained, even if the huge roof seems to reach out beyond the small city lot on which the house stands.

Location
Milwaukee, Wisconsin

Client
Frederick C. Bogk

Date
1916

Main materials
Ferro-concrete, brick

The house of Frederick Bogk in Milwaukee was a project Wright worked on while designing the Imperial Hotel in Tokyo (see pages 38–39), returning regularly from his extended stay in Japan to see the project through. The house owes its appearance to several factors, particularly Wright's interest in the architecture of pre-Columbian America, his work on the Imperial Hotel and the small lot on which he was forced to build. The result was a taller-looking house than Wright usually preferred, set in a conventional position on the lot, with a front garden and a narrow drive down the side of the house.

Standard designs

The project was a challenge for Wright, but he was used to rising to such challenges. More than ten years before designing the Bogk House, he had published a number of house designs in the *Ladies' Home Journal*, part of his campaign to give his work more publicity while also showing that his high standards of design could be applied to houses for people of modest means. These designs were intended to have popular appeal, and were given down-to-earth titles, such as two designs from 1901: 'A Home in a Prairie Town' and 'A Small House, with Lots of Room in It'. Wright also drew groups of these houses, showing how four could be arranged on a single city block, providing plenty of garden space and a pleasant outlook.

One of the later *Ladies' Home Journal* designs was a 'Fireproof House for $5,000'. This was a four-square house with a front featuring two rows of standard-sized windows and a hipped roof, and a plan enabling floors to be made of standard 12-foot (4-m) lengths of timber. The Bogk House is a development of this design, to which Wright brought individuality and refinement.

Visual variations

The street front of the Bogk House has a four-square massing, two rows of windows and a hipped roof (Wright had originally planned a flat roof, reverting to the more traditional hipped design during the design process). But here the similarity with convention ends. The windows, instead of having standard frames, are an artfully arranged collection featuring narrow, recessed openings, glazed with art glass in patterns of small squares. These openings, which look from the outside like tall, vertical slots in the pale brickwork, provide natural light but also offer a degree of privacy because the front of the house is not far from the street.

The pattern of slots of glazing and expanses of brickwork sets up a wonderfully subtle rhythm on the façade of the house, a texture heightened at night when the windows glow with light. The other element in the design is the cast-concrete lintels above the windows. Those above the lower-floor windows have a simple, abstract pattern, but the one above the upper windows is richly ornamented. As well as abstract motifs – in which some observers have seen the architect's triangle and T-square – there are also linear mouldings and what look like stylized faces. The whole composition is a triumph of ornament, showing a strong Mayan or Aztec influence on this Milwaukee street front.

This use of Mayan motifs was important for Wright. He thought and wrote a lot about how architecture should be 'American', and this could mean different things at different times. Often, and rightly, it is taken to mean grounded in the landscape of North America. But Wright also looked to American history, and especially to the great civilizations that had preceded the USA. In Mayan art and

ABOVE Surrounded by houses with conventional, steeply pitched roofs, the Bogk House stands out boldly. From the front, the four-square house looks very simple, but it conceals unlikely spaces – for example, the sloping roof contains an attic, requested by Mrs Bogk so that she could dry her washing without taking it outdoors.

ABOVE The light inside the house has a quality of warmth. This is the result of a combination of factors – tinted glass in the light fittings and in some of the windows, the use of warm colours in the carpets and drapes, and the dark woods of much of the furniture.

architecture he saw sources of a grand and monumental style of architecture, a 'greater elemental architecture than anything remaining on record anywhere else'. In the relatively small Bogk House, he played up this monumentality.

Light spaces The interior rooms are impressively light, especially the dining room, which is at the rear of the house and leads off the living room, the two spaces divided from one another by a short flight of steps. There is a conservatory with pool off the dining room, again a light and pleasant space. The living rooms have recently been enhanced by bringing back the original Wright-designed dining table and chairs, while reproduction Wright furniture is used elsewhere. The living-room carpet is a copy of Wright's original.

Inside and out, the Bogk residence is not what one thinks of as a typical Wright house, but is an impressive response to a stringent set of challenges, which, in the hands of caring owners, has worn well. It also points the way to the more inventive and flexible use of Mayan motifs and patterns in Wright's concrete-block houses of the next few years.

ABOVE Inside, the masonry is even more strongly banded than is usual in Wright's houses. Its striped pattern sets up a rich contrast with the pale ceiling and plain carpets. Some of the architect's built-in furniture can be seen near the fireplace.

Hollyhock House

One of the most surprising of all Wright's houses, Hollyhock House looks from a distance like a strange windowless mass of white concrete. Its pale walls are relieved by repeated cast ornaments, and the building rises like a pale Mayan temple among the surrounding trees. In fact, the house has many windows and the white surfaces are not concrete – this is a building that reveals its true character slowly.

Location
Los Angeles, California

Client
Aline Barnsdall

Date
1919

Main materials
Hollow clay tiles, stucco

Aline Barnsdall was a rich woman with advanced ideas. She was heiress to a fortune made in the oil industry, and passionately interested in the theatre. At some time around 1915 she had the idea of building herself a complex of buildings including a house and an experimental theatre. To begin with, she intended the complex to be in Chicago, but in 1919 she bought a 36-acre (15-ha) site in Los Angeles for the project. The large plot was called Olive Hill, and was indeed a hillside site partly covered by an orchard of olive trees. A keen admirer of Wright's work, Barnsdall was pleased to secure him to do the designs.

Wright took on the job, even though he knew that he would be busy for some time on his biggest project to date, Tokyo's vast Imperial Hotel (see pages 38–39). In the event, Wright spent some five years in Japan, and work on Barnsdall's house went slowly. But an ambitious site plan evolved. As well as Barnsdall's house itself, and its large garage wing, Wright planned the theatre, an apartment building for actors, two directors' houses and a cinema.

From theatre to house
In spite of the client's enthusiasm and large fortune, most of the scheme was not built. The theatre plans fell on stony ground when it became clear that Wright knew nothing about theatre design and, because of his Tokyo commitments, lacked the time to find out. The young designer Norman Bel Geddes, himself working in the theatre at the time, describes in his auto-biography how he tried to challenge Wright about his designs, mentioning European theatres he knew and books about the theatre. But Wright dismissed all this, and persisted in leaving out such essentials as space for scenery or lights. He said he wanted to get back to the essentials of theatre, to produce a kind of theatre that the ancient Greeks would have recognized. But this sounded like bluster, and a way of covering up his ignorance. Perhaps it is fortunate that the theatre itself did not get built. Yet Wright did get his 'ancient Greek' performance space – next to the house is a small semi-circular amphitheatre.

OPPOSITE The living room opens into a loggia and out into this garden courtyard, which is at the heart of the house. On one side of the courtyard (behind the pillars towards the right of the picture) are the kitchen and dining room. Opposite is a long gallery leading to the bedrooms.

ABOVE From the west, Hollyhock House appears as three abstract blocks, representing the central living room with the music room and library on either side. Each reads as a rendered mass, slightly tapering towards the top, and relieved only by rows of cast-concrete ornament in the hollyhock design. Wright referred to this kind of cast concrete by the status-enhancing name of 'art stone'.

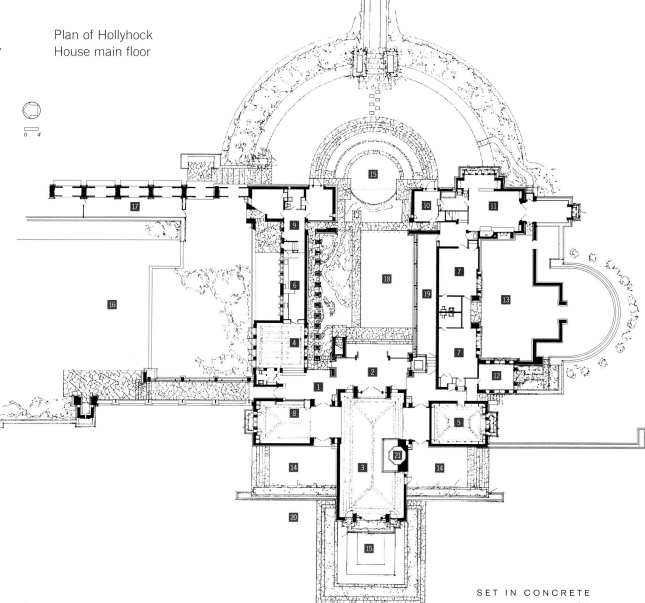

OPPOSITE TOP The centrepiece of the living room is a large fireplace. This is encircled by water, an unusual effect that enabled Wright to introduce another of the four traditional 'elements' (fire, air, earth and water, all essential in truly organic architecture) into the interior of the building.

OPPOSITE BOTTOM The dining room is enhanced by beautiful natural wood panelling and fittings, which are polished to catch the light from the windows. The wood of the table and chairs matches that of the panelling. These are original Wright-designed furnishings, although the house contains others added when the architect renovated the property in 1946.

The house, however, was completed. Wright called it the Hollyhock House, because he incorporated stylized hollyhocks – Barnsdall's favourite flower – into the decoration. Hollyhock House is a new departure for Wright. In spite of its delicately feminine name it is actually a massive structure, with great areas of solid-looking wall punctured by deeply recessed windows and door openings. Only the rows of ornaments – not actually much like hollyhocks, but resembling carvings on a Mayan temple – act as sculptural relief.

A hidden material
All this gives the house the appearance of a massive concrete structure set on its California hillside. Take away this ornament and it could almost be a structure of the 1960s or 70s. But much as it looks like concrete, it is not. The Hollyhock House is actually made of hollow clay blocks, or 'tiles', covered with stucco. Ironically the ornaments are the nearest things on the façades to concrete, and they are made of a form of cast stone.

Wright, though, seems to have wanted people to believe that the house was built of concrete, which was becoming the ultimate 'modern' material. As Wright scholar Robert McCarter has pointed out, the architect labelled the house as being of 'Glass and concrete' in a publication of 1928, and did not correct another writer, Henry-Russell Hitchcock, when he said it was a structure of 'exposed poured concrete' in a book of 1942. So much for the doctrine of 'truth to materials'.

Water and light
Inside the house, Wright once more worked some of his magic with the interplay of spaces. The exterior hollyhock ornament is repeated indoors on large cast-stone columns. And the architect injected an extra dose of magic into the living room's fireplace. This features a hearthstone surrounded by water, so that it seems to float in a pool. Above it is a striking relief made up of blocks of cast stone (an abstract-looking design, although Wright claimed it was a portrait of Barnsdall), and higher still is a skylight, screened with wooden slats. The water in the fireplace 'pool' flows under the floor right across the house, linking two outdoor pools, a memorable merging of indoors and outdoors.

Wright gave woman of the theatre Aline Barnsdall a very theatrical house, in which she could entertain on an impressive scale – dinner guests sitting on tall dining chairs, again designed by Wright. The designs for the house came from the architect through various intermediaries during his absence in Japan. Sometimes his son Lloyd took over the project; sometimes Rudolf Schindler, a young designer who had joined Wright from Vienna and who was probably one of his most talented assistants. The eccentricity, and the curious blend of stylized ornament and faux-concrete, is all Wright's.

RIGHT The plan of Hollyhock House is an unusual one for Wright, combining elements of his favourite outward-looking cruciform plan with an inward-looking courtyard. The living room, music room and library form three arms of the cross and look out over the lawn; the loggia looks the other way towards the enclosed courtyard.

Plan of Hollyhock House main floor

KEY
1. ENTRY
2. LOGGIA
3. LIVING
4. DINING
5. LIBRARY
6. KITCHEN
7. BED
8. MUSIC
9. SERVANTS
10. NURSE
11. NURSERY
12. OBSERVATORY
13. PATIO
14. TERRACE
15. POOL
16. MOTOR COURT
17. KENNELS
18. GARDEN COURT
19. GALLERY
20. LAWN
21. FIRE

La Miniatura

La Miniatura is a small house poised on a sloping site in lush gardens above a ravine. It is the first of a group of houses that Wright built in California using concrete blocks – an unlikely material, to which the architect brought a special character. In this house, the repeating patterns on the blocks interplay magically with the shadows of the surrounding trees.

Location
  Pasadena, California
Client
  Alice Millard
Date
  1923
Main materials
  Concrete blocks

Wright was interested in concrete, and made groundbreaking use of it in the Unity Temple (see pages 32–35). But he was dissatisfied with it as a construction material. This dissatisfaction had something to do with the fact that Wright liked to plan his buildings using a regular grid. He felt that this was a natural thing to do – natural forms tend to crystallize or produce repeating patterns, and modular grids provide discipline and proportion when an architect is laying out the plan of a house.

Wooden frameworks, strips of windows and the repeating patterns of brickwork tend to work well with such a system, as Wright found. Poured concrete, however, does not depend on regular, grid-like patterns. A concrete wall can extend indefinitely, without joints, frames or other structural punctuation.

The cast-concrete block The answer was the concrete block, which Wright could treat as a repeating element. For most, it would not have been an obvious choice because the concrete block was seen as lowly, something used and then covered up, something less attractive than 'natural' materials such as wood or stone. Wright spoke of 'that despised outcast of the building industry – the concrete block' and of the need to rehabilitate it and 'make it live like a thing of beauty'.

So Wright developed a special kind of concrete block. Each block had a groove in each edge, and when the blocks were laid a strand of reinforcing steel was fitted in the grooves to lock the blocks together. The blocks, specially cast to Wright's specifications, could also carry custom-designed patterns, ornament that was an integral part of the structure. It was a system with huge potential.

The Millard House The first Wright building to be constructed in this way was a small house in Pasadena, California, called La Miniatura. It was built for Alice Millard, widow of George Millard – Wright had designed a house for the couple in Highland Park, Illinois, some years before. Alice Millard, persuaded by Wright to buy a sloping site above an arroyo, was delighted with the design for her new house. The plan consists of two squares that meet at one corner. The smaller square contains the garage and entrance loggia. The larger occupies three floors – a lower floor containing the dining room, kitchen and servant's room; a main floor with double-height living room and guest room; and also an upper floor containing Mrs Millard's bedroom. This arrangement makes for a house with a vertical accent, and Wright emphasized this, with tall windows and lines of blocks running from top to bottom of the house. He knew that this precipitous site required a very different approach from his low-lying Prairie Houses.

LEFT All Wright's concrete-block houses make use of the patterns on the blocks to cast strong shadows in the California sun. The effect of the light at La Miniatura is especially beautiful because the surrounding trees and shrubs cast shadows of their own, softening the outlines of the concrete walls.

The interiors are warm and inviting. Although the floors and walls are of concrete, they do not feel cold or harsh because they are polished to a quality finish and visually warmed by good natural light and details such as the wooden-clad ceilings. Surrounded by trees and looking out over water, this is a beautiful house, and both architect and client were pleased with it.

Setbacks
But there were mishaps. A flood ruined the lower floor, the roof leaked and the builder stole materials for another project he was working on. Blaming the builder for the leaking roof, and once-in-50-years freak weather for the flood, Wright found himself mired in lawsuits, arguments and promises to repair the defective roof. He said that he ended up putting $6,000 of his own money into the project, which had already exceeded its original budget of $10,000. But in spite of the problems, Alice Millard stuck by Wright and his architectural vision, and loved her house. And the building has survived the vicissitudes. It is still one of Frank Lloyd Wright's most beautiful houses.

Storer House

After La Miniatura, Wright built a larger concrete-block house for John Storer, a Los Angeles dentist. The building is located on a hillside on Hollywood Boulevard and it stands out, looming above the road, in an imposing, almost self-important way. Next to the road itself is a bulky concrete wall that supports the terrace in front of the house. Behind it, the house itself, with its central row of five vertical strips of glazing – from a distance they look like the windows of five impossibly high rooms – stands tall, looking rather bigger than it actually is.

Location
Hollywood, California
Client
John Storer
Date
1923
Main materials
Concrete blocks

For the Storer House, Wright used his concrete-block construction system, again demonstrating, as he had in La Miniatura, how well suited the system is to building on a steep hillside. But unlike La Miniatura, a rather private house that turns away from the road to overlook its valley, the Storer House overlooks the road, presenting its most dramatic façade to the public.

The house and the landscape
This public face is rather a surprise in a Wright house, not because Wright disliked making big architectural statements – far from it – but because the house seems to stand out from the landscape. In Wright's terms, it seems to be placed *on* the site rather than being *of* it. As Brendan Gill points out in his biography of Wright, this must have been still more obvious when the house was first built. Back in 1923–4 the Hollywood hills hereabouts were sparsely populated and much less built-up than they are today. And there were fewer trees too.

OPPOSITE The tall windows, which light both the dining room and the living room above it, are one of the most notable features of the Storer House. From a distance, most observers do not notice the small interruption in the glass that marks the dining-room ceiling and living-room floor.

RIGHT The Storer House is on three levels and uses its hillside site to full advantage. Seen from the lower level, the various rooms and wings of the house step in and out to make a varied and interesting impression. The façade is further broken up by planting, which Wright allowed for in his plans with the provision of various troughs, beds and planters.

Above the road, the house is dominated by the textured blocks and the tall windows. These high windows are actually divided halfway up. The lower sections light the dining room and can be opened, like French doors; the upper sections light the living room. Wright probably intended that they should 'read' from outside as full-height windows, with the living-room floor floating invisibly behind the glass. But in the event the floor was visible as a small break in the imposing upward expanse of glazing.

Planning for the hillside

The Storer House is built on a T-shaped plan, in the form of a central block with a pair of flanking wings. The central block – standing out at the front because of the tall windows, and slightly higher than the wings – contains the dining room on its lower floor. This doubles as the entrance hall. Above it is the main living room of the house. One side wing contains the kitchen, servant's room, and bathroom; the other houses four bedrooms and two bathrooms.

Behind the house, a series of steps and terraces, held together by Wright's concrete blocks, work their way up the hillside. The blocks work well here, their square form allowing corners to be formed with ease. Wright must have felt that he had hit upon a perfect building system for the steep hills of California, where he was hoping to attract more clients. The striking shape the house makes from the road certainly sends a loud message to passers-by: look at this new kind of house Frank Lloyd Wright can build.

A subtle design

Although the Storer House seems somewhat monolithic and exhibitionistic from the road, it is more successful close-to, when the texture of the concrete walls can be appreciated. Some of the blocks are plain, some have different patterns cast into them, some are pierced. In the sunshine, the light picks up these differences and one can appreciate the subtlety of Wright's design. Although he sometimes spoke of himself as a sculptor, hewing houses out of masonry or concrete, he also liked to use a metaphor of weaving. If the soft surfaces of textiles seem an odd metaphor for a wall made of concrete, the metaphor works in constructional terms, with the bands of steel that hold the blocks together woven through the walls like thread. The notion works visually, too, when we get near the walls and see the varied and changing effects of the sunlight on the blocks. The walls have a rich texture,

LEFT A close-up shows the varied textures of the blocks. The way in which the joins between some of the blocks are recessed recalls the deeply cut joints in the masonry sometimes used in classical and Georgian buildings, an unusual modern take on an old idea.

BELOW The heart of the Storer residence is the central block, which houses the dining room on the lower level and the living room above. This block acts as a core, giving access to the service rooms at one end of the house and the bedrooms at the other.

Plan of entry level

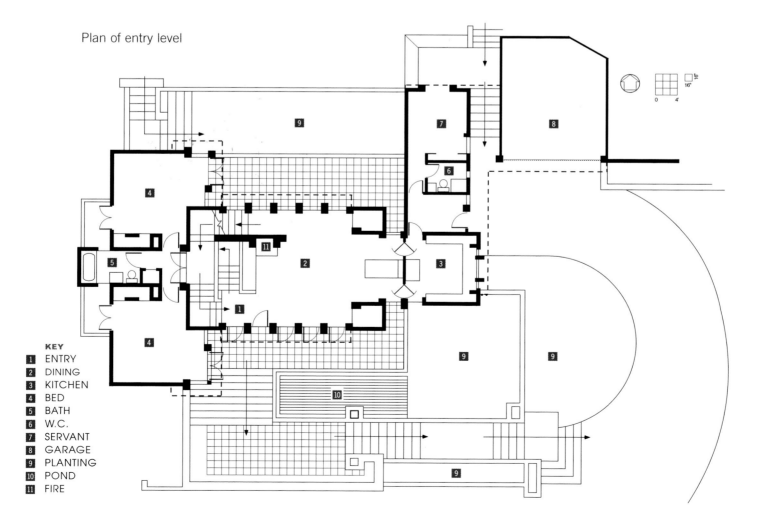

KEY
1 ENTRY
2 DINING
3 KITCHEN
4 BED
5 BATH
6 W.C.
7 SERVANT
8 GARAGE
9 PLANTING
10 POND
11 FIRE

BELOW The texture of the living-room walls is enhanced by quite simple geometrical patterns on the concrete blocks. These patterns are also used on the blocks that make up the balustrade towards the back of the room and on the fire surround, the structure that is towards the right of the picture.

and this is enhanced still further by the shadows thrown across the building by the trees and shrubs that have grown up around it.

Light and concrete also interact to beautiful effect inside the house, where many patterned blocks are used in the inner walls, supporting columns, fireplaces and other features. As well as a rational system of construction, it is possible to see Wright's concrete blocks as a response to the strong but shifting light of Southern California.

Wright believed deeply that what he had designed was a landmark house, and, as usual, went over budget in his attempt to get it right. During the construction period he was much away in Wisconsin, and his son Lloyd, managing the work day by day, often had to make instant decisions. Wright did not always agree with these decisions and had rows with his son, who doggedly continued. Meanwhile the costs mounted and the Storers did not have endless funds. Wright agreed to bear some of the cost of the budget overrun. His need to finish another great building was more pressing than his need to make money. Wright was usually busy, and usually broke.

Ennis House

The Ennis residence is the grandest of Wright's California concrete-block houses. Like its fellows, it makes good use of a hilly site, perched at the top of a rise so that the sun can catch both the texture of the blocks and the complex patterns of the building's masses, windows and walls. A showy and highly visible building, there is no wonder that it has attracted many film-makers over the years.

Location
Los Angeles, California
Client
Charles and Mabel Ennis
Date
1923
Main materials
Concrete blocks

'You see, the final result is going to stand on that hill a hundred years or more. Long after we are gone it will be pointed out as the Ennis House, and pilgrimages will be made to it by lovers of the beautiful – from everywhere.' Those are the words used by Frank Lloyd Wright in 1924 in a letter to Charles and Mabel Ennis, when their house was under construction and things were not going smoothly. Clients, in Wright's ideal world, should try to ignore concerns like schedules and budgets – it would be worth all the trouble and expense in the end, when a perfect and lasting work of art would emerge.

Wright's vision certainly delivered a great house. Another of the architect's California concrete-block houses, the Ennis House is large, monumental and placed on a prominent hilltop site. The site seemed to ask for a big, dominant building, and Wright obliged. Referring to a famous Mayan temple site, Vincent Scully Jr, in his book on Wright, put it like this: 'The Ennis House used its hill as a Mayan temple base and loomed at the top like something from Tikal.' Its pale concrete walls catch the sun and make the building stand out still more.

Patterns of light and space
The building is different on the inside, more reticent and mysterious, parts of it rather dark, but with bits of the concrete walls and piers lit by shafts of light, which also catch the glinting tiles of the fireplace mosaic. Although the basic plan is long and thin, Wright arranged many of the spaces so that one room is entered by crossing another diagonally, meaning that one is more likely to see partial glimpses of rooms than whole vistas. And everywhere the presence of

LEFT This view of the north side of the house shows the monumental effect of the building, with its great masses of masonry. On the upper levels there are only small windows, but lower down there are larger windows, giving the occupants views over Griffith Park.

OPPOSITE Usually in his concrete-block houses Wright mixes patterned and plain blocks in the same wall to give a varied effect. In this part of the Ennis House, however, virtually all the blocks are patterned. The effect really is like the woven textile that the architect often referred to when discussing these houses.

the concrete block – often arranged as piers or expressed as masses that jut from the main expanse of wall – gives an impression of solidity.

The great house was built to last, and found fame, though not quite in the way its architect predicted. As well as featuring in many books about Wright, the house also found a role in the movies. It was seen in *House on Haunted Hill* (1959), *The Day of the Locust* (1975), *Blade Runner* (1982) and a host of other film and TV productions. As a result more people have seen images of this house than of any other Wright building, even though they are not usually aware of what they are looking at.

Fame and misfortune But famous as it has become, the Ennis House has had to

withstand more than its share of wear and tear. The Northridge earthquake of 1994 and the terrible rains of 2005 devastated the house, which was already in a sad way as a result of a less-than-perfect history of maintenance and the deterioration of many of the concrete blocks. A large part of the south wall of the house fell away; the roof needed work; the foundations needed stabilizing; and thousands of blocks (some damaged by water coming through the defective roof, some by attempts at waterproofing that had gone wrong) required replacement.

After the 2005 rains it looked as if the whole building might slide down the hill. By the end of the year the house was on the list of America's 11 Most Endangered Historic Places compiled by the National Trust for Historic Preservation. Wright's claim for a house that would last for a century began

BELOW Wright liked the way that the cubic concrete blocks could be used to create tall piers. As well as supporting roofs or ceilings, these piers give an impression of grandeur, recalling in a modern way the rows of columns in an ancient temple.

ABOVE This route into the dining area of the Ennis House shows an effect common in Wright's buildings – a vista partially interrupted by piers and walls towards a room illuminated with shafts of natural light. The journey from shadows to light was one the architect liked to build into his houses.

BELOW The Ennis House is planned around a central spine that extends from the stairs and living rooms at one end to the long glazed loggia at the other. At one end of this spine are the kitchen and a guest room; at the other the main bedroom with its bathroom. Wright would later develop this kind of in-line plan when building his Usonian Houses.

to look hollow. But the building had its supporters, and soon began to find more, spurred on by publicity from prominent figures such as the actress Diane Keaton. Hollywood began to give something back to the great house on the hill.

Restoration

Since then the work of organizing, campaigning, fundraising, planning and restoring has moved apace. A new structural frame has been installed beneath the motor court, a new south wall built, and a new roof installed. Many concrete blocks were cleaned and repaired but around 3,000 needed replacing, so restorers made moulds of the original blocks and made casts from them, using these new blocks to replace the defective originals. They repaired interior details and took out art-glass windows so that specialists could conserve them. They also undertook all kinds of other tasks, such as painting the kitchen cupboards in their original colours.

The Ennis House now looks as good as it has at any point in its history. A new team of workers, conservators, architects and engineers can now share in the pride of Wright and his original clients. Among those whose pride may be mingled with above-average emotional investment in the project is Eric Lloyd Wright, the architect's grandson, who, having worked on restoration of the Millard, Storer and Freeman Houses, has become an expert in dealing with his grandfather's concrete-block structures. The tradition continues.

Plan of upper levels of main house and chauffer's quarters

KEY
1. ENTRY COURT
2. LIVING
3. DINING
4. KITCHEN
5. GUEST
6. BED
7. BATH
8. LOGGIA
9. CHAUFFER'S BED
10. STORAGE
11. GARDEN TERRACE
12. BRIDGE OVER ENTRY
13. FIRE

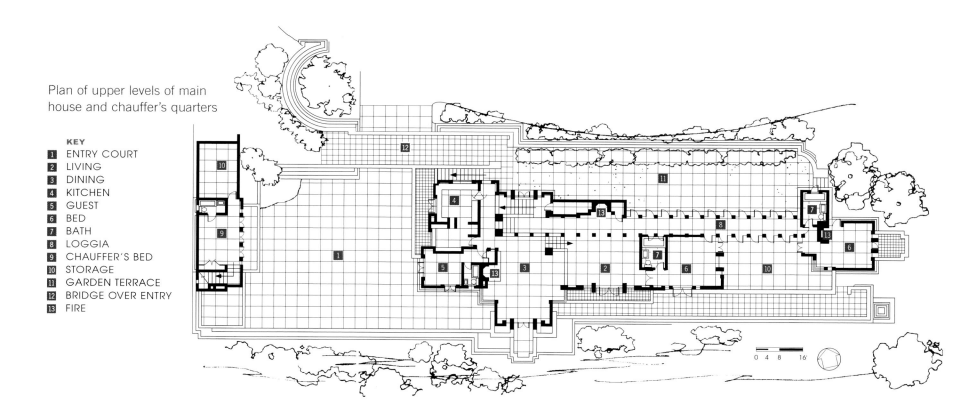

Freeman House

The Freeman House, like Wright's other concrete-block houses, is on a steep hillside site. The hilly terrain among the foothills of the Santa Monica Mountains is reflected in the building's many floors and levels. In the Freeman House Wright added one further key element to the design of the concrete-block house: the use of large corner windows. Combined with pierced concrete blocks, these windows make the lighting of the house especially dramatic.

Location
Los Angeles, California

Client
Harriet and Samuel Freeman

Date
1923

Main materials
Concrete blocks

The house rises through three floors with the living room, kitchen, balcony and garage on the entry level, while the bedrooms and terrace occupy the floor below. Entering the house and walking from the small lobby down the long, narrow hall, you come into the living room at a corner, and crossing the room involves experiencing a strong diagonal.

Effects of the light
Wright employed a particularly dramatic feature in the Freeman House, one to which he was to return in other projects. The Freeman House is the first by Wright to incorporate windows that have no supports or glazing bars at the corners. The panes of glass go right into the corners of the building and are butted together so that they make a perfect joint. In fact these corner windows hardly have any frame at all; the horizontal mullions that hold the glass in place emerge straight out of the block masonry. There is something startling about the juxtaposition of the thin mullions and delicate glass with the massive concrete walls.

The effect of opening up the corners in this way is magical. It extends the view, making house and landscape seem even closer than in Wright's previous interiors. Indeed it seems to dissolve the walls completely, so that you have to look down at the floor or up at the ceiling to remind yourself that you are in a rectangular room. Looking around you, though, you can be in no doubt about the solidity of this building. Massive concrete-block piers and deep ceiling beams sweep across the living room, giving it a very strong sense of structure.

Wright, who liked dramatic effects as much as anyone, no doubt enjoyed the ingenious piece of theatre that makes the corners vanish and renders this house so different from the other concrete-block dwellings that were being built at around the same time. Many have concurred, finding the Freeman House the best of Wright's concrete-block buildings and one of the finest of all his houses.

Owners and houses
The Freemans were in no doubt about the importance of their house either. Samuel Freeman died in 1980, and when Harriet Freeman followed him in 1986 the house passed to the University of Southern California, who have since restored it. Aware that she was owner of an exceptional building, Harriet Freeman ensured that it would remain in caring hands.

Wright's concrete-block houses proved successful and versatile. While Alice Millard filled La Miniatura with antiques, many of which were for sale, the Freemans furnished their house with modern fittings. In his early book on Wright, *In the Nature of Materials* (1942), the architectural historian Henry-Russell Hitchcock stressed how much better it was to furnish the house in a style in keeping with the architect's vision: 'The modern fittings of this house [the Freeman House] produce a more homogeneous effect than the antiques which Mrs Millard kept for sale in "La Miniatura".' In fact the concrete walls and Wright's burnished concrete floors provided a perfect setting for Alice Millard's antiques, which also enhanced the house. There is more than one way to furnish a house, and this fact is a reminder that, modern as they were, Wright's houses – like the works of so many modern masters, from Picasso to Stravinsky – could seem at once both very new and very old.

OPPOSITE The effect of the unusual windows is fully exploited in the living room of the Freeman House. The way in which the glass goes right into the corners opens up a broad vista of 180 degrees, taking in the trees and buildings of Los Angeles. More light comes into the room through pierced concrete blocks, which – with their patterned openings – set up rhythms of light and shade.

LIKE MANY IN THE USA, Frank Lloyd Wright suffered in the Great Depression of the late 1920s. He faced the beginning of the 1930s broke, with little work, and his taste for a lavish lifestyle unabated. Tradesmen were demanding payment of bills, and the architect needed all his powers of inventiveness to see him through.

One of his first solutions to his problems was to create a new organization, the Taliesin Fellowship. He invited people to apply to become his apprentices. In return for a fee and a commitment to a fixed amount of manual work on his Wisconsin farm, Wright offered 23 men and women the chance to learn architecture from the master and to assist him in the projects he was working on. The apprentices lived on Wright's property, Taliesin, took their meals together and observed fixed hours of work, recreation and sleep. The income from the fees helped turn Wright's finances around, and for the rest of his life Wright was short of neither support nor assistance.

As the 1930s progressed, Wright began to turn his practice around too. Major commissions came in the form of the headquarters building for the Johnson Wax Company in Racine, Wisconsin; a house for Herbert Johnson of Johnson Wax; and his most famous house of all, Fallingwater, the residence poised over a waterfall in Pennsylvania. Landmark projects like these proved excellent publicity and brought Wright to the attention of many new clients.

Most of these clients wanted more modest, less costly houses than Fallingwater, and Wright, always conscious of the market for houses for 'middle-income' people, developed the low-cost 'Usonian House'. This kind of house brought the benefits of a Wright-designed residence – practicality, open-plan living rooms, an organic unity of house and site – to many professionals, bringing lots of work to the architect's practice and increasing his influence. After unpromising beginnings, the 1930s proved to be Wright's most successful decade after the Prairie House years of 1901–10.

A NEW
BEGINNING

ABOVE In the huge drafting room at Taliesin, the roof trusses rest on inverted wooden triangles supported in turn on small stone piers. No architect working here could fail to be reminded of the structural ingenuity of Frank Lloyd Wright, and of the way in which Wright could make interesting shapes and patterns out of his structures.

OPPOSITE Frank Lloyd Wright works on a drawing with some of his apprentices in the drafting room at Taliesin. An apprentice would produce a drawing, which would then be altered or corrected by Wright in a continuous process of development and refinement, during which the student would absorb the wisdom and techniques of the master.

Taliesin Fellowship Complex

The Taliesin Fellowship Complex is the group of buildings that Frank Lloyd Wright designed to house his community of young architects, who came to live, to learn, and to assist him at Spring Green, Wisconsin. Together these buildings form a living memorial to a unique way of teaching and practising architecture. Fittingly, the big drafting room with its complex roof trusses – spiders' webs of beams and braces – is the most memorable structure on the site.

Location
Spring Green, Wisconsin

Client
The architect

Date
1932

Main materials
Stone, wood

In 1932 Wright turned 65. He did not have as much work as he had had a few years earlier, because the Depression of the late 1920s had meant that there were fewer clients around with money to spare. Many men in his position would have considered retiring, but Wright decided to make a new beginning. He founded the Taliesin Fellowship, an organization that would allow him to take on a number of apprentices, and he built a home for the fellowship on his family land at Spring Green, Wisconsin.

The apprentices of the Taliesin Fellowship came to learn from the master and to assist him in his work. They would draw up plans for imaginary projects, and Wright would criticize them in the most hands-on way. As the Wright scholar William Allin Storrer has written: '… each apprentice would draw his idea of a good American home; Wright would rework the student sketch, breathe life into it, and thus help the student develop his skills.'

The life of the Fellowship
But this was no ordinary architectural training. The students lived on site, at Taliesin, and took part in the day-to-day jobs that needed doing about the place. The way of life has been compared to that of monks in a monastery. The buildings that Wright designed for the Fellowship in some ways reflect this. The main Fellowship building contained the drafting studio – a large, open-plan room where all the students sat and drew – and 16 small rooms for the apprentices. These apprentice rooms are placed either side of the drafting room, along its long sides, in two rows of eight.

The drafting room
The extraordinary roof that Wright designed for the drafting room is one of its most memorable features. It is supported on a series of complex wooden trusses, each of which rests on wooden equilateral triangles with one angle pointing downwards and standing on a stone bearer on the floor. The design of the trusses allows for a row of north-facing clerestory windows in the roof, and the trusses also have a pronounced slope from one wall to the other, accommodating another long window under the higher edge of the roof. So from the inside, the impression is of a sloping roof supported on a web of intersecting timbers, from between which spreads a gentle north light.

Because the roof is supported by its triangular frameworks, the walls of the room seem to float free of it. Unlike so many rooms, where the walls are the main feature and carry the structure, here the roof is the main element, together with the large fireplace at one end, which acts as a focal point. It is a reminder that this room is in a way also a domestic space. For all the rows of drafting tables and the serious work that went on here, it was also the heart of the complex, the place the apprentices called home.

From the outside, this dramatic building is part of a complex of structures that Wright built on the site, some earlier, some later than the drafting room. In addition to Wright's house (see pages 72–75), these include a theatre, originally completed shortly after the drafting room but later destroyed by fire and rebuilt. But the drafting-room building, with its striking sloping roof, stands out from the other structures with their hipped and flat roofs.

Fallingwater

Perched above a stream in southwest Pennsylvania, Fallingwater is one of the landmarks of 20th-century architecture. Its daring structure, apparently floating above a waterfall, creates a perfect marriage of setting and building, Cantilevered balconies provide views through the trees, and, inside, natural rock seems to have pushed its way through the floor to form the central hearth. This close union of place and structure makes Fallingwater both an outstanding embodiment of Wright's ideas about organic architecture and one of the best-known houses in the world.

Location
Bear Run, Pennsylvania
Client
Edgar J. Kaufmann
Date
1935
Main materials
Reinforced concrete, stone

'Come along, E.J. We're ready for you.' One Sunday morning in September 1935, Edgar J. Kaufmann, owner of Kaufmann's store in Pittsburgh, was about to make the two-hour drive to Wright's home and headquarters at Taliesin, Spring Green, Wisconsin. Nine months previously, Kaufmann had commissioned Wright to build him a new house by a stream in the Appalachians. Now the architect was inviting his client over to look at the sketches. But there weren't any sketches. Wright put down the telephone and picked up his pencil. In the two hours it took Kaufmann to arrive, he had made a series of rough drawings of the building that was to become the most famous modern house in America. After nine months of gestation, Fallingwater was born.

Design and structure
Wright liked to stage tricks like this. He knew very well that the story of how he created these drawings would get back to the client – after all, one of his apprentices at Taliesin was none other than Kaufmann's son, also called Edgar. But if it looked like a conjuring trick, Wright's daring two-hour drafting session for the Kaufmann house also had a more serious side. Wright said that he liked to think about a building, to get it clear in his head, before putting his ideas down on paper. He liked to let the building 'live' in his mind, 'gradually taking more definite form before committing it to the draughting [sic] board'. It was a remarkable skill, involving holding the site and all the elements of a building – the spaces, the materials, the structures – clearly in the mind and refining them.

Of course, this dramatic revelation of the architect's ideas was just the beginning. There followed months of detailed site surveys, structural assessments, and more precise plans. Kaufmann was pleased with the plans – but worried about the structure. Could the house safely balance above the waterfall the way the architect proposed? The storeowner sent the plans to his own structural engineers, who raised more doubts. Wright, who after all had an engineering background, was livid when he found out that his expertise was being questioned. He offered to pull out of the project completely if he had lost the trust of his client. Kaufmann backed down, and let Wright follow his instincts, his training, and the structural expertise of his team.

OPPOSITE Perched above its waterfall and surrounded by rocks and trees, Fallingwater has one of the most stunning locations of any house. Wright rose to the challenge of this site with a combination of vertical stone walls, horizontal concrete balconies and strips of glowing light from the windows.

RIGHT A pale concrete exterior stair is superimposed on one of the natural stone walls, the regular steps of the balustrade standing out against the rough grey masonry. Wright relished this diversity of materials, adding an unusual element of strong colour to the mix in the form of red-painted window frames.

Building and setting
When Fallingwater was complete, Kaufmann saw that his trust had been rewarded. A series of cream concrete terraces are cantilevered out over the waterfall, facing in different directions to take advantage of the moving sun and the views. They seem to float by magic over the rocks and the stream, tied together by a contrasting central section of stone, a vertical element that balances the horizontal terraces. Between the terraces, bands of windows blur the boundary between indoors and out, and glow with light after dusk.

The result is remarkable. The concrete terraces, which ought to look alien in this environment of rocks, water and trees, seem to grow out of the landscape, and Wright was so proud of the appearance of the house from across the stream that he had steps cut in the rock to form a viewing platform from which

ABOVE The combination of natural and artificial patterns and materials continues inside the large living room. The ceiling and the window frames display ordered patterns of rectangles, but Wright contrasted these rectilinear elements with the natural irregularity of the stone floor. Sections of stone wall (far right) continue this theme.

visitors can take in the whole house. What they see – stone walls echoing the natural rock beneath, concrete terraces, and roof planes spreading left and right – is a breathtaking union of structure and place.

The relationship of land and building was crucial for Wright. He said that 'While [man] was true to earth his architecture was creative'. Just as his low-slung Prairie Houses had been true to this dictum of organic architecture, hugging the land and looking out in all directions, Fallingwater kept faith in a different way with the organic ideal. It is not only that the house seems to grow out of its setting, apparently emerging from the rocks and woods of Pennsylvania. The building is organic inside, too. In the house's largest space, the vast but low-ceilinged living room, occupants are aware all the time of the surroundings. The room's long windows offer views of trees in almost all directions, and the rocky terrain seems to encroach indoors – literally so near the fireplace, where bedrock boulders push their way through the flagstones of the floor. Opening a door on to one of the terraces brings birdsong and the sound of the waterfall right into the house. The great outdoors and the great indoors meet and merge triumphantly.

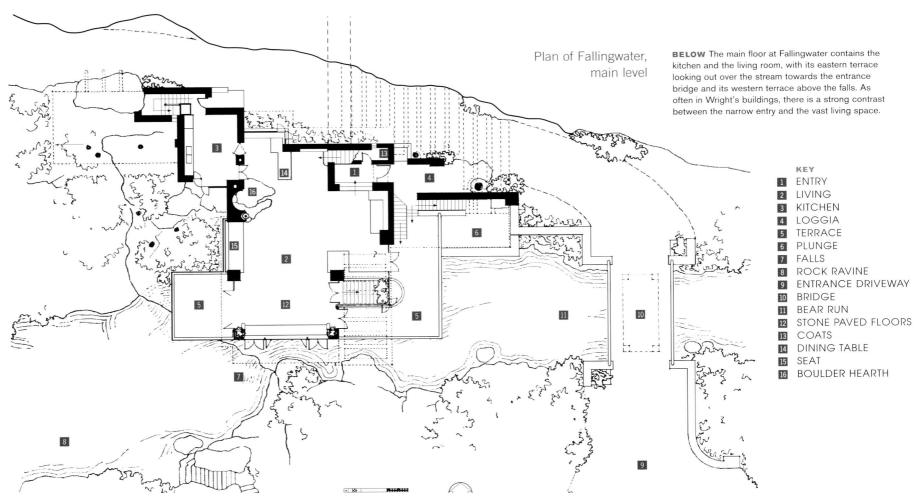

Plan of Fallingwater, main level

BELOW The main floor at Fallingwater contains the kitchen and the living room, with its eastern terrace looking out over the stream towards the entrance bridge and its western terrace above the falls. As often in Wright's buildings, there is a strong contrast between the narrow entry and the vast living space.

KEY

1. ENTRY
2. LIVING
3. KITCHEN
4. LOGGIA
5. TERRACE
6. PLUNGE
7. FALLS
8. ROCK RAVINE
9. ENTRANCE DRIVEWAY
10. BRIDGE
11. BEAR RUN
12. STONE PAVED FLOORS
13. COATS
14. DINING TABLE
15. SEAT
16. BOULDER HEARTH

First Jacobs House

In the 1930s, Frank Lloyd Wright developed a series of houses for middle-income clients. These small, innovative houses became famous, and the Jacobs House at Madison, Wisconsin was the first. It combines a compact plan with an inexpensive, mostly wooden structure, and proportions that give the building a simple elegance. Wright used similar elements in other house designs, and they were widely influential and much imitated by other architects.

Location
Madison, Wisconsin

Client
Herbert Jacobs

Date
1936

Main materials
Brick, wood

In the mid 1930s Herbert Jacobs, a newspaperman from Madison, Wisconsin, issued a challenge to Frank Lloyd Wright: design and build me a house for $5,000. Wright was known, of course, for large, elaborate houses and some of his clients were very rich; but throughout his life the architect also thought of ordinary, or at least middle-income, Americans. In the early years of the 20th century he produced a series of designs for inexpensive homes, which were published in magazines. Now, in response to Jacobs' challenge, he turned again to the question of good-quality house design for the ordinary American. He came up with an economical timber-framed structure on which he would play scores of variations during the rest of his working life.

Usonian Houses

Wright called these buildings 'Usonian Houses'. There has been some debate about the origin of this word. Wright himself said that the British writer Samuel Butler had called the USA 'Usonia', and Americans were therefore 'Usonians'. In the early 20th century there had also been talk about calling the USA 'USONA' (United States of North America) to distinguish it from the new Union of South Africa, but some preferred 'Usonia' as sounding more harmonious.

Whatever the precise origins of the name, Wright saw his Usonian Houses as quintessentially American buildings. They mostly had several features in common. They were usually small buildings without the big garages and service wings of the larger Wright houses. They were often L-shaped, but these 'L's had arms of varying lengths, so that they would fit on irregularly shaped plots, which were often cheap. A lot of wood was used in their construction. They had flat roofs, overhanging generously to provide shade – often the overhang was extended to form a carport. They benefited from plenty of natural light and had underfloor heating. Above all, they sat comfortably in their environment, as all the architect's houses tended to do.

Another key element of the Usonian Houses was the use of a grid plan. Wright usually used grids in planning his buildings, but they were especially important in the Usonian Houses, for various reasons. Wright carefully chose a 2-foot x 4-foot (60-cm x 120-cm) module for the Jacobs House. This corresponded to the size of the components of the building, saving construction costs. The grid was also visible in the sections of the concrete floor, so that the builders could easily see where the walls needed to go.

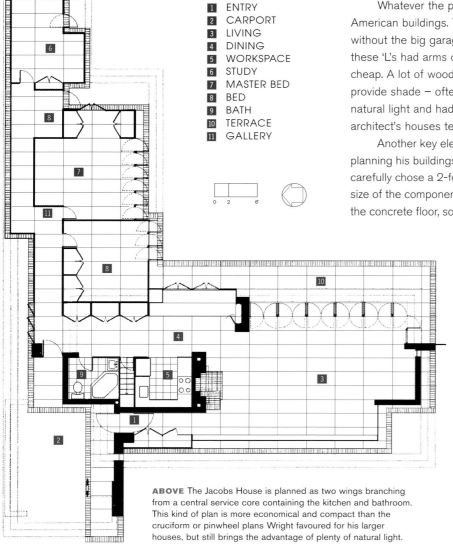

KEY
1 ENTRY
2 CARPORT
3 LIVING
4 DINING
5 WORKSPACE
6 STUDY
7 MASTER BED
8 BED
9 BATH
10 TERRACE
11 GALLERY

ABOVE The Jacobs House is planned as two wings branching from a central service core containing the kitchen and bathroom. This kind of plan is more economical and compact than the cruciform or pinwheel plans Wright favoured for his larger houses, but still brings the advantage of plenty of natural light.

ABOVE Herbert Jacobs needed plenty of space for books, and Wright accommodated shelves along the back wall of the living room. The distance between the shelves is the same as the width of the timbers that clad the wall, so proportions as well as practicality are served here. Wood also makes a big impact on the living-room ceiling, adding a touch of richness to this otherwise simple house.

OPPOSITE This view of the back wall of the Jacobs House living room shows how much of the structure of the building is timber, but with sections of brick at key points, such as the end wall and fireplace. The emphasis is on simplicity and economy, a formula that proved attractive to many of Wright's middle-income clients.

Structural concerns
Wright responded creatively to Herbert Jacobs's request. He used a mainly wooden structure. The walls had a core of plywood sheeting, which Wright covered on either side with a damp-proof membrane. The builders screwed battens to this core and these supported the cladding of pine boards, which lined both the inner and outer walls, eliminating the need for plastering and painting. This sandwich-like timber framework became a hallmark of the Usonian Houses, although instead of pine Wright later used cypress wood.

A certain amount of brick was also used in the structure, and there was a rumour that Wright tried to keep costs down by 'siphoning off' some of the bricks from the Johnson Wax Administration Building (see pages 112–115), which was under construction at the same time as the Jacobs House.

The decluttered plan
The house was planned simply, with good use of the L-shape. One wing contained the large living room and the other housed the bedrooms. At the corner, where the two wings joined, was a 'service core' built of brick and containing the entry, bathroom and kitchen. Although compact, the house feels spacious. This is because it is well planned and also because Wright included built-in furniture, shelves and closets, which encouraged the owners to restrict clutter. The underfloor heating also eliminated radiators, saving more space and reducing expense further by avoiding the structures used to hide radiators in some houses. Economy and simplicity went hand in hand.

Paul and Jean Hanna House

Like many of Wright's California houses, the Hanna House makes good use of a hillside site, with plenty of big windows to take advantage of the view and several terraces looking out over the garden at different levels. A striking feature of the house is that few of the walls meet at right angles because the plan is based on a hexagonal grid, a design idea that Wright took from one of his apprentices, Cornelia Brierly.

Location
Stanford, California

Client
Paul and Jean Hanna

Date
1936

Main materials
Wood, brick

A love affair with our house: these were the emotional terms in which Paul and Jean Hanna described their feelings about their unique home. And their emphasis was on the 'love' – the relationship lasted most of their lives, and survived a vast budget overrun and changes in family size and needs. The Hannas were committed to their house, and it repaid their huge financial and emotional investment.

Plans and budgets Paul Hanna, a professor at Stanford University, commissioned the house from Wright in 1936, the time when the architect's star was rising again as a result of projects like Fallingwater and the Johnson Administration Building. Wright's reputation was for lavish houses like Fallingwater, but he was also developing the concept of the less-costly Usonian House (see pages 106–107) at this time, so took on the Hanna House at a budget of $15,000. True to form, the costs spiralled and the finished house cost the Hannas some $37,000. This must have been a blow to a man on a salary of $4,400, but the Hannas persevered.

The couple crossed swords with Wright, as clients tended to do. They had various clashes over details of the design, but their greatest panic occurred when they discovered that the site of the house was directly over a fault. In this earthquake zone this was worrying, to say the least. But when the couple contacted Wright, he wired back, 'I built the Imperial Hotel.' They should not worry. But such detachment is not always easy in California.

However, the Hannas felt they had a house worth the money. In many ways it was the typical modern Wright house the couple wanted, with a spacious well-planned interior and a stunning use of the site – a hillside location, to which the house clings, its various levels and terraces making satisfying use of the terrain. They felt too that the open plan created a series of rooms that would encourage a creative, nurturing atmosphere, ideal for bringing up their children. They were not the first to fall for the congeniality of the typical Wright house.

The 'honeycomb house' But in one way the Hanna House was a surprise, representing a new departure for the architect. Most buildings are based on rectangles. They have rectangular plans, rectangular rooms and rectangular walls. Wright had always been interested in breaking free from the hold of the rectangle. From the start of his architectural career he had added semi-circular bays to his rooms and experimented with rooms of unusual shapes, such as the octagonal library in his first home in Oak Park. By using spaces that interpenetrated, he was also breaking free of the rectangle in many of his later houses. The Hanna House breaks free of the rectangle by being based on a grid of hexagons. Soon after the plans were drawn, people began to refer to it as the 'honeycomb house'.

The slab floor of the house is made up of hexagons with 26-inch (66-cm) sides (26 inches/66 cm is also the distance between the vertical studs in the timber walls). The house walls – both the outer walls and the partition walls between rooms – follow the lines of the sides of these hexagons; so while the

LEFT The fireplace, with its recessed hexagonal grate, marks the boundary between living and dining spaces, and heats both. The chimney and flanking walls form part of the only bulky mass of masonry in the house, the rest of the structure being made up of thinner brick walls and large glass windows.

ABOVE The southwest-facing living rooms of the Hanna House open on to a long terrace that is partly sheltered with overhanging roofs and trees so that the occupants can enjoy both sun and shade. Hexagonal planters are a reminder of the unusual, six-sided planning grid on which the house is designed.

rooms themselves are not hexagonal, their walls do not meet at right-angles. As in the Usonian Houses, the use of this standard grid made the wooden walls of the house more straightforward to build (although there are also some walls made of brick). The timber partition walls were also easy to remove or adapt, so in 1957, after the Hanna's children had grown up, the couple altered their house, removing some of the partition walls to make larger living spaces. Wright, then aged 89, oversaw the alterations.

The later history of the house During the 1960s and 70s, the Hannas transferred the ownership of their house to Stanford University, originally intending it to be used to accommodate some of the distinguished academics who come to the university as visiting professors. For some years Stanford used the building as its Provost's House, until in 1989 disaster struck, in the form of a major earthquake. The quake badly damaged the foundations of the house, and had it gone on any longer would probably have brought down the fireplace, chimney and roof. The university began a full restoration, improving the foundations in the process.

  The house is now used as a venue for special university events, including dinners and seminars, and is also opened to the public so that visitors can appreciate the special atmosphere in which Paul and Jean Hanna lived for nearly 40 years. They can understand at first hand the paradox of this house – that it seemed to achieve something akin to perfection in its original form, but that it could also withstand alteration as its owners' requirements changed, demonstrating perhaps another aspect of organic architecture – its power to adapt over time.

RIGHT This corner of the living room shows clearly how the whole design of the house is based on hexagons. As well as the floor slabs and the angle of the walls, even the specially made furniture, with its six-sided cushions, reflects this theme. Wright often mirrored structural and decorative details in this way.

BELOW This long living room, with its dramatically sloping ceiling, is marked 'playroom' on plans of the house, but makes an ideal space for a long dining table from which diners can look out on to the terrace and beyond. Wright built in a long seat for relaxation too.

Plan of house as originally built

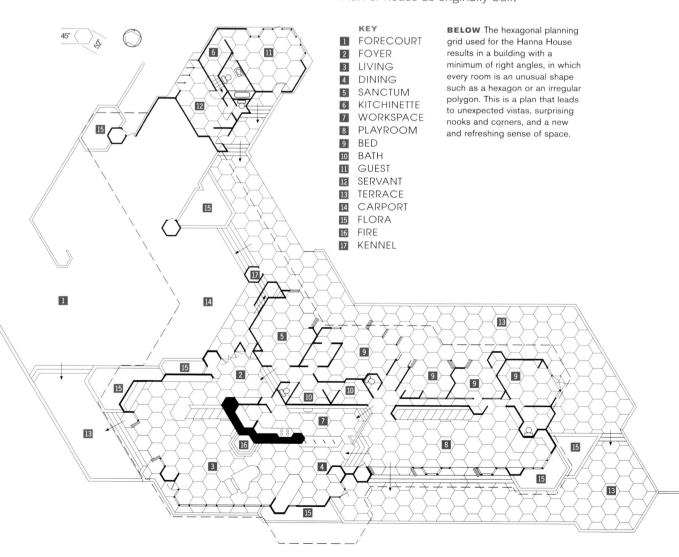

KEY
1. FORECOURT
2. FOYER
3. LIVING
4. DINING
5. SANCTUM
6. KITCHINETTE
7. WORKSPACE
8. PLAYROOM
9. BED
10. BATH
11. GUEST
12. SERVANT
13. TERRACE
14. CARPORT
15. FLORA
16. FIRE
17. KENNEL

BELOW The hexagonal planning grid used for the Hanna House results in a building with a minimum of right angles, in which every room is an unusual shape such as a hexagon or an irregular polygon. This is a plan that leads to unexpected vistas, surprising nooks and corners, and a new and refreshing sense of space.

SC Johnson and Son Company Buildings

The Administration Building for the Johnson Wax Company is one of Frank Lloyd Wright's greatest structures. The large, open-plan space is dotted with unique concrete mushroom-like columns that support the ceiling, creating one of the world's most striking office interiors. It is a strong building from the outside, too, and all three of its main materials – the concrete of the columns, brick and glass – are used in unusual ways in this landmark structure.

Location
Racine, Wisconsin

Client
Herbert F. Johnson Jr, president, Johnson Wax Company

Date
1936, 1944

Main materials
Brick, concrete, Pyrex glass

Johnson Wax was one of America's largest privately owned companies. It manufactured floor-care products, the wax that polished millions of American floors, and its products and marketing were good enough for it to have pulled out of the Depression by the mid 1930s. As the firm expanded, company head Herbert Johnson knew he needed a new office building. His organization had always treated its workers well – his was the first American company to share profits with its staff – and he wanted a building that would be comfortable to work in. He commissioned an architect called Matson to design the building, but the rather conventional drawings Matson came up with failed to inspire him. Then Johnson's general manager, Jack Ramsey, went to see Wright.

A visionary appeal

Ramsey was bowled over by the architect's visionary approach and introduced his boss to Wright. At first, the two men found it difficult to agree. It is said that the only thing they had in common was their taste in cars – both owned new Lincoln Zephyrs, the latest in streamlined automotive design. But with the strong backing of Ramsey, Wright won the commission. It was the beginning of a friendship that, surviving many arguments and setbacks, created two of Wright's greatest structures, on the headquarters site of Johnson's company in Racine – the great brick-and-glass Administration Building, which Wright designed in 1936, and the later Research Tower of 1944. Both are landmark buildings.

Just as he had done 30 years earlier in the Larkin Building (see pages 30–31), Wright came up with a radical design concept for a demanding client. The roof, much of it a latticework of glass, is held up by some 60 reinforced concrete columns, which Wright described as dendriform (tree-shaped) but others have compared to mushrooms. These tall columns are very narrow at floor level, gradually widening until they reach the upper part of the vast double-height space that is the main workroom of the office building. At the top they broaden out into discs. The glazed spaces between them glow with light.

Testing the columns

Work on the building proceeded quickly until the authorities questioned the structural soundness of Wright's columns. According to Wisconsin building codes, a concrete column designed to hold 6 tons should be 30 inches (75 cm) in diameter. But the Johnson columns were only 9 inches (23 cm) across at the bottom. Arguments went back and forth until the

RIGHT The exterior of the Administration Building gets its effect from the use of curves at the corners and from the different materials. Contrasting bands of red brickwork and windows mark the exterior, with an added accent of light from the pale coping stones at the tops of the walls.

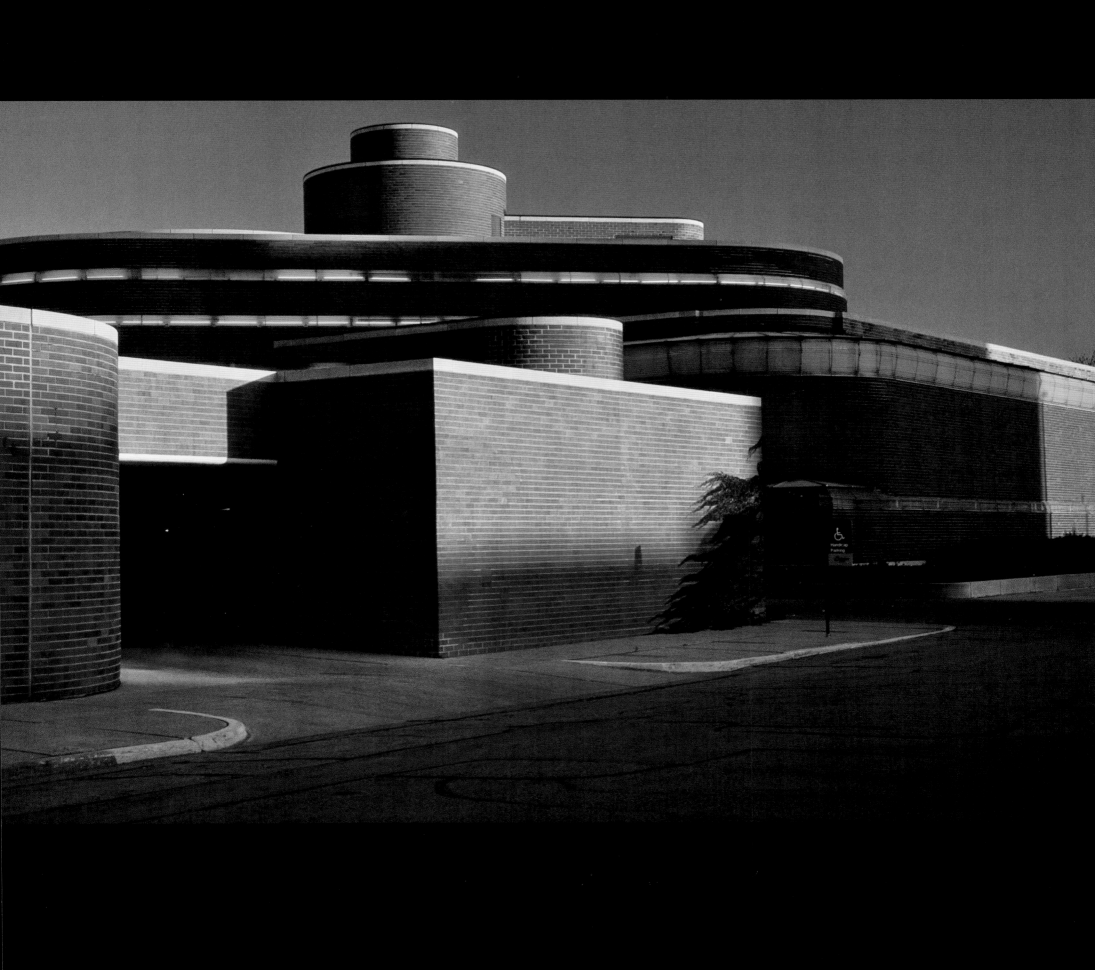

ABOVE The famous workroom interior of the Administration Building is a forest of tree-like, or mushroom-shaped, concrete columns. The space is filled with furniture designed by Wright, which originally included three-legged chairs that were designed to fall over if users did not sit on them with the correct posture.

Wisconsin Industrial Commission finally agreed to resolve the issue by allowing Wright to build a column and test it by loading it with sandbags.

On the day of the test, workmen, architects, Taliesin apprentices, engineers, clients, bureaucrats and the press gathered round to watch a crane load sandbags on to the flat top of the 'mushroom'. As the load reached 12 tons, the bureaucrats of the Industrial Commission declared they were satisfied and the press, who were hoping for a dramatic collapse, looked disappointed. But Wright blithely told the crane operator to carry on loading the column. Loading continued until the column was holding 60 tons, at which point the top broke but the column remained defiantly standing. The point had been made.

The glazing was Wright's other major innovation. To fill the spaces in the ceiling between the column tops, and for the band of glazing that went around the upper part of the outer walls, Wright used not flat glass but tubes made of Pyrex glass, the material used for test tubes and heatproof containers. No doubt this choice of rows of tubes appealed to both Wright's and Johnson's love of streamlining. Some commentators have also pointed out that it let in the light while denying the workers a view out. This had two advantages – the staff would concentrate on their work and would not be reminded of what Wright saw as the uncongenial suburban district that surrounded the building (he had hoped to persuade Johnson to build on a new, out-of-town site).

The Research Tower
Johnson came back to the architect for a building to house his company's research laboratories. Wright had always wanted to build a tower on the site, to balance the long, low Administration Building, and seized the chance, coming up with a design in which the floors are cantilevered out from a central, stem-like support, so that the outer wall could be a non-structural 'skin' made up of Pyrex glass tubes and narrow bands of brick. The tower also has rounded corners, mirroring the shape of the Administration Building.

Sadly, the tower was never the success that Wright and Johnson hoped. Its internal rooms are too hot and sunny for comfort, and – because Wright refused to install ugly sprinklers – experiments involving combustible materials had to be carried out in a different building. From the outside, though, it still looks good next to its more practical sibling.

RIGHT This close-up of a walkway in the Johnson complex shows the use of Pryex glass tubes. Wright liked these because they let in the light while obscuring the view out. This walkway shows how the round tubes were also well suited to creating a curved surface without any of the challenges involved in bending plate glass.

ABOVE Wingspread is an unusual Wright house, its high roof line soaring above rows of windows and large areas of siding. The design of the highest feature, the observation tower, is reminiscent of the brick-and-glass buildings Wright built for Johnson Wax, the company run by Wingspread's owner, Herbert F. Johnson.

Wingspread

One of Frank Lloyd Wright's largest houses, the 14,000-square-foot (1,300-sq-m) Wingspread was designed for Herbert Johnson of the Johnson Wax Company. This big house is centred on a vast central living room with a stepped octagonal roof. The four main wings 'pinwheel' out from this central feature, their red-brick walls and low profiles reaching out into the extensive grounds, near Lake Michigan. A house of big vistas and grand rooms, Wingspread also has intimate spaces and a surprisingly warm atmosphere.

Location
Wind Point, Wisconsin
Client
Herbert F. Johnson
Date
1937
Main materials
Brick, stone, wood

In the late 1930s Herbert F. Johnson, having divorced his first wife, was preparing to remarry. He needed a new family house, with enough space for his two children and those of his new wife, and he turned to Wright, who was already working for him designing the new Johnson Wax Administration Building (see pages 112–115). Although in some ways Johnson was frustrated by Wright, whose delays and escalating fees were as bad as ever, he knew the architect would produce a great design. The client's confidence was justified – the house, which Wright named 'Wingspread', was one of the grandest and most memorable of his career.

The pinwheel plan

Most of Wright's largest houses were based on either cross-shaped or pinwheel plans, giving the architect the scope to 'zone' the building in four distinct wings. Wingspread, a huge pinwheel, is no exception. Each of the four wings has its role: one for the kitchen and servants, another for the children's bedrooms and playroom, a third for the guest rooms and a fourth for the master bedroom. Each wing takes full advantage of the many outside walls, with views in several directions and access to terraces, balconies or pergolas – for example, the children's rooms open on to the terrace where the swimming pool is located, while the master bedroom has its own upper terrace.

At the heart of all these wings is the central living room, a large 40-foot x 60-foot (12 m x 18 m) octagon topped by Wright's grandest domestic ceiling. This corbels its way up at the centre in four stages, each with its own row of clerestory windows throwing light into the space below. In the centre, rising right up through the heart of this space, is a huge brick chimney serving a cluster of fireplaces that heat the living spaces around it.

Although this central space is conceived as one great volume – Wright referred to it as 'the wigwam' – it is actually made up of four separate living areas: a large living room, a dining area, an inglenook and a small library. Each focuses on a fireplace while also looking out through windows towards gardens or terraces. Wright-designed furniture completes the picture.

One piece of furniture attracted special notice. This was a dining table that was designed to slide away into the adjacent serving area, where the servants could set down the food and then slide it back again. Apparently, the idea was that even the successive courses of a formal meal could be served in this way. But the sliding table had its drawbacks. Guests could be left holding their cutlery while their food vanished from in front of them, and in the end the sliding table was replaced. It was one innovation too far.

RIGHT Rows of roof windows light the high central living space that forms the heart of Wingspread's pinwheel plan. All the main areas of the house, from the children's wing to the kitchen and serving area, lead from this imposing space, which is exquisitely finished with wooden panelling and high-quality brickwork.

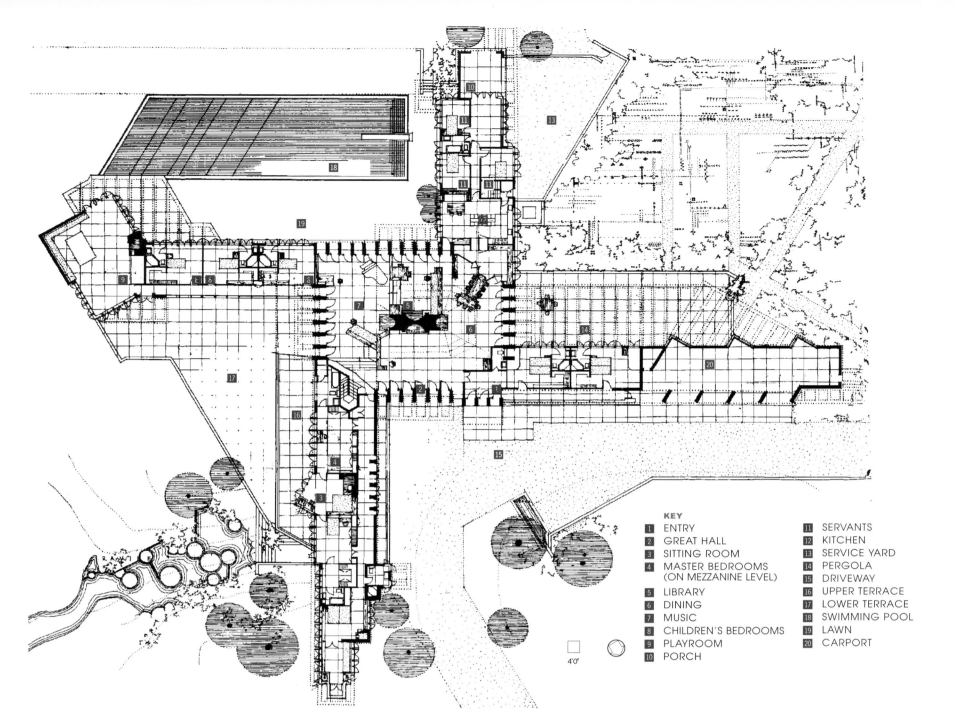

KEY

1	ENTRY	**11**	SERVANTS
2	GREAT HALL	**12**	KITCHEN
3	SITTING ROOM	**13**	SERVICE YARD
4	MASTER BEDROOMS (ON MEZZANINE LEVEL)	**14**	PERGOLA
5	LIBRARY	**15**	DRIVEWAY
6	DINING	**16**	UPPER TERRACE
7	MUSIC	**17**	LOWER TERRACE
8	CHILDREN'S BEDROOMS	**18**	SWIMMING POOL
9	PLAYROOM	**19**	LAWN
10	PORCH	**20**	CARPORT

ABOVE This is one of Wright's most ambitious plans, a pinwheel, in which each arm of the cross is offset from the central core. As well as dividing up the house, this kind of plan also creates four separate outdoor spaces between the wings – an area for the pool, a quieter terrace off the bedrooms, the entrance area and a service court.

RIGHT This tall fireplace is set in the middle of the central living space, and is thus at the very heart of the whole house. To one side a spiral staircase winds up towards the observation tower, its protective metal railings mirroring the shape of the semi-circular hood above the fireplace.

ABOVE The lower ceiling in part of the living area allows for a mezzanine level above. Features like this enabled Wright to vary the quality and size of the spaces inside this large house. Walking around Wingspread therefore involves experiencing a series of visual surprises – although there is also visual unity, arising from the use of the same materials (brick, cypress wood and sandstone) throughout the house.

Materials and surfaces
Wingspread is beautifully built in pink sandstone, red brick and cypress wood. These natural materials were handled with great skill and sensitivity by the master builder, Ben Wiltscheck, and Wright was impressed in particular with the brickwork, which he judged the best in any of his buildings. The bricks were made specially and the mortar treated with special care. By having the vertical mortar courses tinted red and the horizontal courses deeply raked, Wright achieved his usual goal of a horizontal emphasis.

He also treated the floors with care, staining concrete slabs red and using plywood for some of the floors. Once again, he was taking commonplace materials that most people looked down on or thought best for industrial applications, and giving them special treatment.

An organic house?
Wingspread imposes itself on the landscape much more forcefully than most of Wright's smaller houses. The roof of the central living space rises high, and still higher is the glass 'observatory' tower that Wright designed to rise out of it. So although much of the building is low, like the typical Wright organic house, the building is more dramatic, and feels like a house imposed on the landscape.

Nevertheless, Wright saw his great house for Herbert Johnson as an example of organic architecture. He pointed to the natural materials, from sandstone to cypress, and to the way that, as usual, house and surroundings are integrated. He also said that the house improved the site – modesty was never Wright's strongest character trait.

Even Herbert Johnson found the house somewhat grand, but lived in it for around 20 years before handing it to a charitable foundation as a conference centre. This involved a certain amount of conversion work – for example, turning the garages into offices – but the heart of the house has been preserved so that it can be enjoyed by conference delegates and visitors alike.

Taliesin West

A desert building, made partly of 'desert masonry': this was Frank Lloyd Wright's formula for Taliesin West, his Arizona winter base. Massive blocks of local stone held together in a matrix of concrete make up much of the masonry, while Wright lightened the effect with canvas roofs, which were designed to let in both light and air. The structure therefore combined mass and lightness, the permanent and the temporary, in a way unheard of in previous American architecture.

Location
Scottsdale, Arizona
Client
The architect
Date
1937
Main materials
Desert masonry, wood, fabric

Wright loved the Arizona desert. He found the rocky, empty terrain inspiring when he visited it in the 1920s, and when, after he had been ill with pneumonia, his doctor suggested a winter relocation to a hotter environment, the architect jumped at the chance to build a new winter base there. He chose a site on the Maricopa Mesa near the McDowell Mountains. Although it is now partly surrounded by the suburbs of Scottsdale, there is still enough of the desert environment left to preserve the atmosphere and sense of place that Wright must have experienced when he first went there. It was a place that had once been inhabited by Native Americans; a boulder decorated with Native American marks was found on the site and erected proudly near the entrance. Wright liked the fact that his new winter base had been inhabited long before.

RIGHT The drafting room, with its huge eleven-section roof, is the largest space at the Taliesin West complex. The main slope of the roof, seen here beyond the pool, faces southwest, so the panels of canvas that originally covered it filtered the bright afternoon sun to create a softer light for working.

Workplace and home

The new residence, which Wright called Taliesin West, was a winter home for the Taliesin Fellowship, so it had to provide a drafting room and rooms for the apprentices and staff, as well as a house for Wright. In addition, there were workshops, since Taliesin West was a hands-on place and was actually built by Wright and the apprentices, and altered, extended and adapted by them over the years. The basic plan was one of Wright's L-shaped designs, with the drafting room along one wing, the apprentices' rooms on the other, and private accommodation for the architect, his wife, and their daughter at the junction. There was also a long loggia, linking the drafting room with the private rooms, as at Taliesin (see page 101).

As ever, Wright wanted to make the building true to its environment. First and foremost, this meant creating what Wright referred to as 'broken lines' – a jagged outline, because the desert itself had no unbroken straight lines. The architect also wanted to use desert materials, but use them in a new way. The builders gathered local stones from the site, placed them in wooden forms, and then poured concrete into the forms to make a solid mass of what became known as 'desert masonry'. When the wooden forms were removed, Wright had the builders chip away the thin layer of concrete on the outside to reveal the stones within, sometimes washing the surfaces of the stones with acid to reveal their colours even more strongly. The result was solid masses of masonry in which large stones appeared trapped in the concrete.

A new kind of roof

Wright used desert masonry for the lower walls of Taliesin West, but added a very different kind of structure on top of this massive base. This superstructure consisted of a series of timber frameworks with linen canvas stretched over them. It made the building seem like a tent, with the fabric letting through lots of light but not glare, and with numerous flaps, blinds and cords, so that entire areas of what would normally be wall could be folded away to open the interior to the air. In addition, the canvas covering coped well with the desert climate. But it needed regular renewal. Wright knew this, and meant the renewal of the canvas roofs to be part of the annual ritual of the move to Taliesin West in the winter.

Architect and apprentices worked on the building in other, more permanent ways, too, adding a theatre in 1949 and a 'Music Pavilion' in 1956 to accommodate the expanding activities – especially social events – of the Fellowship. These buildings are set near the entrance to the complex and do not interfere with the bold shapes and broken outlines of the drafting room and the other original buildings.

Later changes

Sadly, though, there have been other changes, further from the spirit of Wright's original conception. The annual task of renewing the canvas roof covering was later rejected in favour of a labour-saving plastic roof, which still diffuses the light but has none of the airy, breathable quality of the original fabric. This alteration means that the interiors are more enclosed – more like conventional interiors, in fact. Wright's original scheme with the fabric panels and flaps meant that large parts of the interior could be opened to the outside, reflecting Wright's concept of the place as a 'winter camp' and taking the integration of building and landscape just about as far as it could go.

Architects still learn their skills at Taliesin West, which continues as the base of the Taliesin Fellowship as well as being home to the Frank Lloyd Wright Memorial Foundation. The buildings are opened to the public, so everyone can see Wright's achievement and learn about the continuing work of the Fellowship.

OPPOSITE TOP Although large masses of desert masonry are used in places, the main impression created by the large studio living room is one of lightness. The windows, with their views out, and the masonry, with its stones imported from the desert, bring indoors and outdoors together.

OPPOSITE BOTTOM In the open-plan drafting room, Wright could move at will from one desk to another, correcting or improving the drawings of his apprentices and assistants. Even now that the roof covering has been replaced, the room still has something of the atmosphere of a very large tent.

Annie Pfeiffer Chapel

'A great education temple in Florida': these were the words with which Dr Ludd Spivey, President of Florida Southern College, attracted Frank Lloyd Wright to design a group of new buildings for his Methodist college. The most prominent is the Annie Pfeiffer Chapel – a tall building, its pale walls leading the eye up to a prism-like tower. This eye-catching tower is topped not with a conventional spire, but with an unusual openwork metal structure, making the chapel a true landmark.

Location
Lakeland, Florida
Client
Florida Southern College
Date
1938
Main material
Concrete blocks

BELOW The chapel interior shows how Wright used structure to provide visual interest. The openings in the wall and the patterns made by the glazing bars in the large window both encourage one to look up and make an important contribution to the quality of the space.

Wright created a master plan and designed 18 structures for the campus, of which 12 – including administration, science and library buildings and two chapels – were built. Together, the architect's buildings for the Florida Southern College comprise the largest group of Wright-designed buildings in the world. The Annie Pfeiffer Chapel, named for Annie Merner Pfeiffer, a philanthropist who devoted both time and money to church charities, was the first of this unique collection of Frank Lloyd Wright buildings to be constructed.

Chapel and setting
Although Wright was hired because of his devotion to organic architecture, when it came to the chapel he did not want to create a building that stayed close to the ground. The chapel soars. And yet even this pale concrete building with its tall concrete-and-steel tower was designed to fit into its surroundings. The site was dotted with citrus trees, and Wright planned the structure so that the main part of the walls – the section of the elevation that is pale concrete – would be concealed by the leafy canopies of the trees. The visitor would see the concrete-block-built lower part between the tree trunks, and the tall tower ascending towards the sky, but the bulk of the walls would merge with the tree canopies. Most of the trees no longer stand, so the chapel looms larger than the architect intended.

A light interior
Inside, there is also a soaring quality to the space. In plan, the building is rather like a theatre, with an expanse of seating and a raised 'stage'. The main volume is hexagonal, but two rectangular transepts protrude from the long sides of the hexagon, to provide more seating. There are

further seats on upstairs balconies above both the transepts and the rear of the main volume. Originally the entire student population of the college (up to 800 people) could be accommodated; now that the college has some 1,800 students, this is no longer possible.

Around and above the seats, light pours into the chapel from two kinds of opening. Up above there are large areas of clear skylight, while further illumination comes through small openings in the lower walls, which are pierced with panels of coloured glass. So white and coloured light enters the chapel from all angles, and bounces off the interior walls, balcony fronts and other surfaces. It is an impressive and inspiring effect.

The landmark tower
Rising still higher is the chapel's unusual tower. This is a curious composition made up of concrete prisms and hexagons, topped with a grid of steel that has been likened to a bicycle rack high in the sky. It makes the chapel into a clear landmark, and perhaps this was in Wright's mind. This being a college with a Christian foundation, he no doubt wanted the chapel to be a physical focus on the campus.

The parents and sponsors who funded the campus buildings were probably surprised at this strange chapel. And yet, with its tower, the Annie Pfeiffer Chapel is rather more like a conventional place of worship than Wright's Unity Temple of more than 30 years before (see pages 32–35). Annie Pfeiffer herself reacted ambiguously to the finished building: 'They say it is finished,' she said. This made Wright roar with laughter, but he preferred a more uplifting outlook. He saw the Florida complex as growing 'out of the ground and into the light, a child of the sun'. The place has been known as 'Child of the Sun' ever since.

Schwartz House

Among the articles written by Wright to popularize his ideas about architecture, and showcase house plans, was one in *Life* magazine in September 1938. This featured a house 'For a Family of $5,000–$6,000 Income'. The Schwartz House in Two Rivers, Wisconsin, follows the design closely. This Usonian House, built of cypress wood and brick, is a good example of Wright applying his theories in practice – and creating an attractive home in the process.

Location
Two Rivers, Wisconsin

Client
Bernard Schwartz

Date
1939

Main material
Wood, brick

One of the people who saw Wright's article in *Life* was a Wisconsin businessman called Bernard Schwartz, who wanted to build a house near the East Twin River at Two Rivers, Wisconsin. He went to see Wright, and soon architect and client had agreed to build a house based on the published design.

The house is built to a T-shaped plan. The living space, opening on to a terrace, is set along the upright of the T – as usual with Wright, this is by far the largest room in the house. Wright refers to it in his plan as a 'recreation room' and includes, at one end of it, a more intimate corner space, with seats built around the walls, marked 'Lounge'. The crosspiece of the T contains the rest of the rooms. On the first floor these are the dining room (which opens directly off the recreation room), the kitchen, the utility room and the master bedroom with its bathroom. Above these rooms is a second floor with a further group of bedrooms and bathroom.

The house plan
The planning is slightly unusual for a Usonian House, in that Wright's usual principle was to have all the rooms near the ground on a single floor. But although there are three bedrooms upstairs, the master bedroom is downstairs, so Schwartz and his wife spent most of their time on the lower level, living close to the ground.

Outside, on one side of the living room and next to the master bedroom, is a sunken courtyard. On the other side of the living room the original *Life* plan placed a swimming pool. This is omitted in the finished Schwartz House, the only principal difference between the published and built plans. The house is set at an angle to the plot, to take full advantage of the views.

Bricks and boards, light and shade
Inside and out, the house is constructed of a harmonious combination of brickwork and cypress wood, the latter used in the form of boards and battens. The brick is used for the piers between the recreation room French windows, for the fireplaces and for the kitchen. Elsewhere the boards predominate. They are also used to clad the ceilings, and in the recreation room there are several different ceiling heights, which break up the large space and allow clerestory windows to bring additional light between the boards.

As usual, Wright was especially exercised with the play of light and shade. The house has many floor-to-ceiling windows, and these fill the rooms with light – in the recreation room, the pattern created

LEFT In the foreground is the living room (marked 'recreation room' on the plans) of the Schwartz House, its south-facing side consisting of a row of brick piers framing four pairs of French windows. The handling of the masses of brick and the flat planes of the roofs is simple but masterly.

by strong light through the windows and bars of shadow thrown by the brick piers can be dramatic. More subtle are the patterns of light admitted through the strips of clerestory window used in the house. These windows, running along the tops of walls and between ceilings of different levels, are treated in a special way, their glazed openings cut from the wood with a fretsaw to make repeating patterns.

Kitchen and living space

One interesting aspect of the plan, shared by several of the Usonian Houses, was the position of the kitchen. It was traditional to place the kitchen next to outside walls, with views out. But in the Schwartz House the kitchen is tucked between the utility room, dining room and stair, with the entry via the recreation room. Wright wrote about living space and kitchen positioning in his *Autobiography* (words he reprinted in the book *The Natural House*). These were the first two requirements in planning a Usonian House:

1 We must have as big a living room with as much vista and garden coming in as we can afford, with a fireplace in it, and open bookshelves, a dining table in the alcove, benches, and living-room tables built in; a quiet rug on the floor.

2 Convenient cooking and dining space adjacent to if not a part of the living room. This space may be set away from the outside walls within the living area to make work easy. This is a new thought concerning a kitchen – to take it away from outside walls and let it turn up into overhead space within the chimney; thus connection to dining space is made immediate without unpleasant features and no outside wall space is lost to the principal rooms.

The Schwartz House conforms to most of these principles, with the exception of proximity to the chimney – in this house the chimney is diagonally across the recreation room from where the kitchen is sited. But the lack of outside walls and direct access to the dining room are both maintained. So are the key features of the living room – the fireplace, good views, built-in furniture and shelving, and so on. The resulting spaces are both inviting and practical.

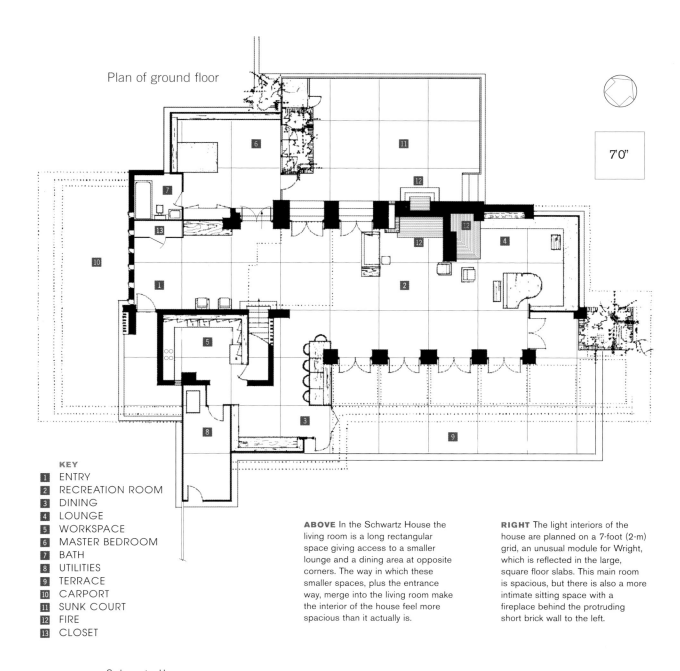

Plan of ground floor

70"

KEY
1 ENTRY
2 RECREATION ROOM
3 DINING
4 LOUNGE
5 WORKSPACE
6 MASTER BEDROOM
7 BATH
8 UTILITIES
9 TERRACE
10 CARPORT
11 SUNK COURT
12 FIRE
13 CLOSET

ABOVE In the Schwartz House the living room is a long rectangular space giving access to a smaller lounge and a dining area at opposite corners. The way in which these smaller spaces, plus the entrance way, merge into the living room make the interior of the house feel more spacious than it actually is.

RIGHT The light interiors of the house are planned on a 7-foot (2-m) grid, an unusual module for Wright, which is reflected in the large, square floor slabs. This main room is spacious, but there is also a more intimate sitting space with a fireplace behind the protruding short brick wall to the left.

Lewis House
130

Lewis House

The challenge of building on a flood plain stimulated Frank Lloyd Wright to produce one of his best Usonian Houses. The main part of the Lewis House is raised above the entrance and carport to keep it free of possible flood water and to give good views towards the river. It is an ideal marriage of house and site.

Location
Libertyville, Illinois

Client
Lloyd Lewis

Date
1939

Main material
Wood, brick

All his life, Wright liked sloping sites. He encouraged some of his California clients to choose 'problematic' lots for their houses, relishing the way he could combine his engineering and architectural skills to make the buildings cling to the hillside or seem to emerge from the scenery. Some of the concrete-block houses had been conceived like this, and Fallingwater was the ultimate in this kind of building.

Floating houses Although the Usonian Houses were intended to be simpler and cheaper to build than these more ambitious projects, Wright played a variation on the Usonian plan that drew inspiration from some of these more dramatic houses. Known as the 'floating' or 'raised' Usonians, these buildings make use of a main floor poised above a low-level entry, carport or service rooms.

When Wright was approached by his friend Lloyd Lewis, editor of the *Chicago Daily News*, to plan a house for him, this was the kind of design the architect chose. Both Lewis and his wife Kathryn were journalists. They had a large circle of friends, including many in the literary world, and liked to entertain. They wanted a house with some grandeur and space, but on a budget.

Above the water The raised layout was especially appropriate for the house at Libertyville because the site was on the flood plain of the Des Plaines River. Wright planned to build on a slight ridge parallel to the river, so it made sense to put the main rooms on an upper level, away from possible flood water. Only the carport, servant's room and guest room are downstairs.

The main rooms are laid out in a version of one of Wright's standard Usonian plans. This is known as an 'in-line' plan, in which the rooms are arranged in one long row, with kitchen and dining room at one end;

RIGHT The wooden ceiling of the living room is pitched – a surprise in this house of flat planes and straight lines – to give a feeling of generous space. A strip of clerestory windows lets in extra light, too, to make this an inviting space during the day, while built-in light fittings illuminate the room by night.

OPPOSITE Raised above the flood plain, the living room and terrace of the Lewis House look out through the trees. The house, built mainly of wood, works well in combination with the surrounding tree trunks, while the red paint of the terrace screen adds a little extra interest as well as visual warmth.

living room in the middle; and two bedrooms, each with its own bathroom, at the other end. The living room has a row of glazed doors opening on to a spacious screened terrace – an essential for Wright because the room is on a higher level than the garden, and without the terrace there would be no direct access to outside space.

One slight break from the in-line plan is a small room, labelled on plans variously as 'study' and 'sanctum', which is accessed from the living room and has a balcony protruding from the rear of the house. The layout gave Lewis the best of both worlds: a generous living room, ideal for the large parties he liked to throw, and a small private room where he could work – or simply retreat – in some privacy.

Privacy – and convenience – was also important when it came to the bedrooms and bathrooms. Each bedroom, including the guest and servant's rooms, has its own bathroom. Wright was thoughtful about bathroom provision. In his summary of Usonian principles in his *Autobiography*, he was pragmatic, including a single bathroom not directly connected to any one bedroom. He held the view that 'Bathrooms opening directly into a bedroom occupied by more than one person or two bedrooms opening into a single bathroom have been badly overdone.' Lloyd and Kathryn Lewis got the more luxurious option of a bathroom for each bedroom.

As in the Schwartz House (see pages 126–129) and other Usonians, Wright employed a mix of brick and timber. The timber was used in an especially creative way in the ceilings, where in some places the boards, instead of all running in one direction, run parallel with each of the four walls, like a series of concentric picture frames. Some are also left with gaps between them, so that hidden lights can shine through.

The river environment
Outside, another unusual touch is that the terrace and the balcony off the 'sanctum' are protected by screens. Wright did not normally favour screens, which he no doubt felt interrupted the sweeping lines of his walls and terraces. Here, though, a riverside setting with a vigorous insect population made screens a necessity. With their red metal supports, they form an integral feature of the design.

The proximity to the river was the whole point of the house, but it got client and architect into an argument about the view. Lewis was annoyed when he discovered that the wooden parapets of the terrace were too high for him to see the river when sitting down. Couldn't Wright remove one of the cypress boards? Wright refused, knowing that this would ruin the design, and wired Lewis, threatening to pull out of the project. The architect followed up his telegram with a more temperate – but still firm – letter, pointing out that you could still see the river when sitting at the dining table. Lewis relented, accepting the design: 'Your letter was swell. Your letters are always swell. It's your telegrams that are lousy. I guess mine are too.' Architect and journalist made up, and Lloyd Lewis remained one of Wright's favourite clients.

Plan of main (upper) floor

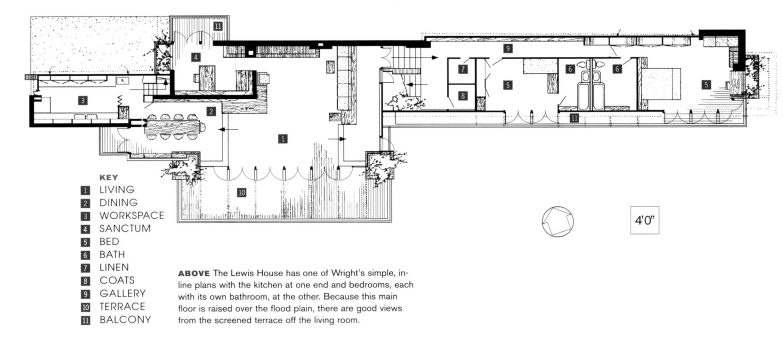

KEY
1 LIVING
2 DINING
3 WORKSPACE
4 SANCTUM
5 BED
6 BATH
7 LINEN
8 COATS
9 GALLERY
10 TERRACE
11 BALCONY

4'0"

ABOVE The Lewis House has one of Wright's simple, in-line plans with the kitchen at one end and bedrooms, each with its own bathroom, at the other. Because this main floor is raised over the flood plain, there are good views from the screened terrace off the living room.

Pope–Leighey House-

The house that Wright built for the newspaperman Loren B. Pope in many ways represented the perfect match of house and client. Pope was a thoughtful man who recognized that a house has a spiritual as well as a physical side, and Wright responded to his wishes with a simple but elegant Usonian House, perfectly matched to its setting.

Location
Falls Church, Virginia
Client
Loren B. Pope
Date
1939
Main material
Cypress wood, brick, glass

Loren Pope worked as a copy-editor for the *Washington Evening Star*. When he read an article about Fallingwater, he knew he wanted to live in a house by Frank Lloyd Wright. So Pope wrote to Wright to ask the architect to design him a house, and in his letter the newsman showed that he appreciated how there is more to a building than bricks and mortar. The things a man wanted out of life, wrote Pope, include both 'Material things and things of the spirit. The writer has one fervent wish that includes both. It is a house created by you.' That was on 18 August 1939. By November, the plans were off the drafting board and, as building began the following summer, Pope began to see his wishes coming true.

A house on a budget Wright did not always produce drawings so soon after being commissioned. A large house such as Fallingwater or the Darwin Martin residence needed a long gestation. But Loren Pope did not have the money of a Kaufmann or a Darwin Martin – his job on the *Evening Star* brought him just $50 a week. When he found it hard to get a loan to pay for the unconventional house, his generous employer took pity on him and advanced him the $5,700 that he needed to build the place and pay the architect's fee.

So the house Wright built for Loren Pope was a simple variation on the economical Usonian model, and did not take long to design. It has an L-shaped plan with one wing deeper than the other, one of a group of houses by Wright that followed this kind of layout and which are sometimes known as 'pollywog' (or 'tadpole') Usonians. This is a layout that enabled the architect to place the bedrooms in a separate wing, offering privacy, while giving both bedrooms and living spaces a view of the garden.

The entry, at the meeting point of the two wings, leads to a short flight of five steps down to a foyer area with the kitchen on the right, the dining room to the left, and the living room, focused on its fireplace, straight ahead. The dining room has glass doors opening on to the garden, while the adjacent living room opens on to a terrace facing in the opposite direction; so, as usual with Wright, entry is through a shadowy foyer into a space flooded with light. But this light was softened by shade. Originally there was a large tulip tree in the garden, and this provided dappled shade as one looked out of the dining-room windows. A number of other trees surrounded the building, and Wright drew these carefully on the plans to indicate the shade and also the gap between two trees that framed the view from the terrace.

The use of cypress boards for most of the exterior blends well with the environment for which the house was originally designed, and the horizontal timbers, flat overhanging roofs and single-level layout

OPPOSITE In this and many other Usonian Houses, Wright used a novel method of letting in extra light. Wooden panels were cut with a fretsaw in repeating patterns and glazed. This gives an additional texture to the wooden panelling in the house, and the pierced panels are used both in vertical strips and in horizontal bands at the tops of walls.

ABOVE This view of the Pope–Leighey House, its wooden siding blending beautifully with the fallen autumn leaves, shows the end of the bedroom wing in the foreground, with the living-room wing to the left. The projecting flat roof to the right is the carport, Wright's answer to the question of how to house an automobile in a low-cost house.

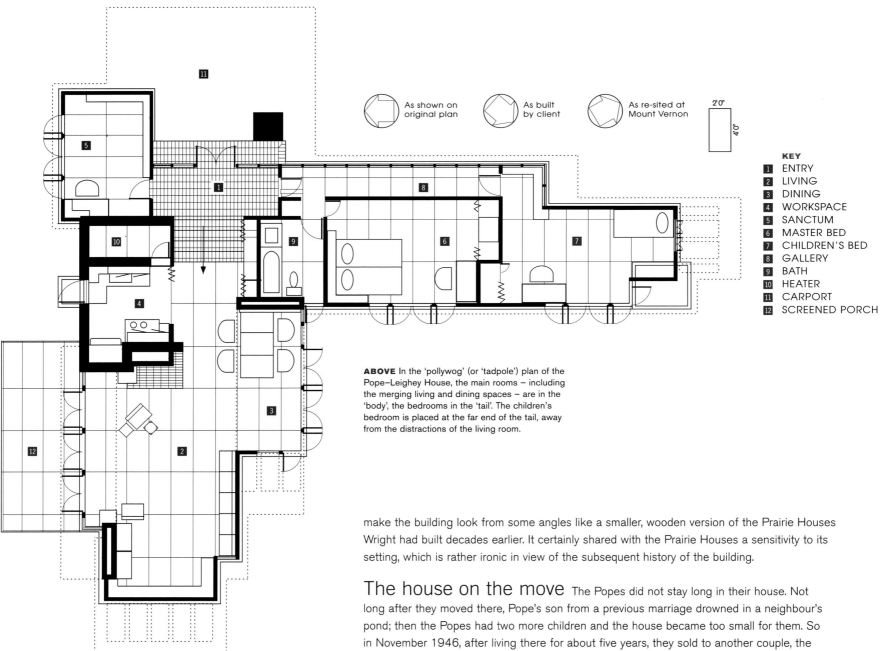

As shown on original plan

As built by client

As re-sited at Mount Vernon

20'

40'

ABOVE In the 'pollywog' (or 'tadpole') plan of the Pope–Leighey House, the main rooms – including the merging living and dining spaces – are in the 'body', the bedrooms in the 'tail'. The children's bedroom is placed at the far end of the tail, away from the distractions of the living room.

make the building look from some angles like a smaller, wooden version of the Prairie Houses Wright had built decades earlier. It certainly shared with the Prairie Houses a sensitivity to its setting, which is rather ironic in view of the subsequent history of the building.

The house on the move

The Popes did not stay long in their house. Not long after they moved there, Pope's son from a previous marriage drowned in a neighbour's pond; then the Popes had two more children and the house became too small for them. So in November 1946, after living there for about five years, they sold to another couple, the Leigheys, and left. Pope said that on the day they moved he sat by the house's all-important fireplace and wept.

The Leigheys stayed much longer than the Popes, and so the building is now usually known as the Pope–Leighey House. But after Robert Leighey died in 1963, the Interstate 66 highway was extended nearby and the building was in its path. Marjorie Leighey did not want to see her house demolished, so she offered the building, together with its furniture, to the National Trust, and they accepted, permitting Mrs Leighey to remain as a lifetime tenant – she lived in the house until she died in 1983. But the house had to be moved, and in 1964 the building relocated to Mount Vernon, Virginia.

This was only the beginning of the saga, however. On its new plot, the house was not oriented according to Wright's plans (in fact, even at Falls Church it had not been set in precisely the position Wright had intended). Then the new foundations began to crack and the decision was made to move the house again, to a site uphill. Once more it was incorrectly oriented and once more the foundation was unstable. The Trust embarked on another restoration, at last ensuring that this small but beautiful Wright house is preserved.

OPPOSITE The bedrooms in the Pope–Leighey House are not large, but Wright compensated for their small size by providing built-in furniture. This includes closets, some with space-saving concertina doors, and items like this dressing table, with its large wall-mounted mirror, a feature that also makes the room feel more spacious.

Goetsch–Winckler House

The house that Wright built for Alma Goetsch and Katherine Winckler, two
instructors at Michigan Agricultural College, is a simple but beautiful composition
of planes and surfaces, and is one of Wright's most successful Usonian Houses.
Dominated by a large, light living space, the house – clad in cypress boards –
looks out over its tree-covered setting, of which it seems a natural part.

Location
Okemos, Michigan

Client
Alma Goetsch and
Katherine Winckler

Date
1939

Main material
Cypress wood, brick

No Wright house is a building in isolation. All the architect's
buildings relate sympathetically to their surroundings and are meant to
promote a particular way of life – one in which people and families live
in harmony with one another, with the environment and with the
elements. Wright also hoped to house entire communities in his
buildings, bringing this way of life to millions.

One such community nearly materialized in Lansing, Michigan,
where a group of faculty members of Michigan Agricultural College
(now Michigan State University) banded together to buy a site on
Herron Creek, not far from the campus. Here they intended to build
seven houses, and commissioned Wright to do the designs. But there was a problem. When Wright
submitted his plans to the Federal Housing Authority, they were rejected. Wright was angered to be told

LEFT The Goetsch–Winckler House is one of the simplest and most minimal of all the Usonian Houses. It gets its effect from the happy composition of walls and overhanging flat roofs, and from the way that it lives up to Wright's dictum that a house should be 'of' its environment rather than imposed on it.

that the walls would not support the roofs, that the underfloor heating was impractical, and that the unusual designs would make it difficult for owners to sell their houses if they chose to do so. For the potential owners, this meant that banks would not provide finance, and the scheme collapsed.

A house among trees

But one of the houses went ahead anyway. This was for two female members of the faculty, Alma Goetsch and Katherine Winckler. Wright designed a house of great simplicity and beauty, poised in typical Wright fashion on a ridge. Entering the house, you pass through one of a row of glazed doors into the studio and living room. The windows of this living space look directly out over the ridge, so that the house seems suspended among the trees, a delightful effect. To the left of the entry is the kitchen, to the right the bedrooms – it is a very compact plan for a small house built for two women of modest means.

The other remarkable feature of the house is the pure beauty of the way Wright balanced the different masses that make up the rooms, and the various flat planes that are the roofs. The Goetsch-Winckler House, small but beautifully formed, is a wonderful example of Wright's compositional genius.

Floating next to its surrounding trees, the Goetsch-Winckler House has stood the test of time well. In fall especially, when the leaves come down and their browns and oranges blend satisfyingly with the red brick and brown timber of its walls, the house could not look more 'grounded'. Indeed, as the surrounding trees have grown it seems still lower, as if clinging to the earth. The Federal Housing Authority need not have worried about its structural integrity either (although, to be fair, the overhanging carport roof has been reinforced with additional structural steel). Although small, it is one of the architect's most perfect creations.

Wright must have known this, and his anger with the FHA's reaction to his plans rumbled on for years. It became public again in January 1948, when an issue of *Architectural Digest* was given over entirely to Wright. Among the designs published in the magazine, Wright included the scheme for the Michigan houses, adding a text that fulminated against the FHA's decision. Since they threw out his designs, Wright noted proudly, Usonian Houses had been built in 29 states. They had not fallen down, their underfloor heating worked, they pleased their owners. The proof of the pudding, Wright implied, was in the eating. The government official had not only made a mistake, but had missed the opportunity to endorse a kind of housing that was especially appropriate to North America. The Usonian House was here to stay.

BELOW From the living room, this view looks towards the alcove sitting space with its fireplace; to the left of this is the small kitchen. Clerestory windows are used all around the house, to provide plenty of light and to highlight the texture of the ceiling. Wright-designed furniture completes the picture.

THROUGHOUT HIS CAREER, Frank Lloyd Wright courted controversy, and the architect often found himself going against the grain of those around him. The last phase of his working life, from the closing years of the Second World War to his death in 1959, found him continuing to come up with new ways of designing buildings, some of which proved to be just as controversial as his early works. A number of these late buildings have been criticized by architectural writers, who consider that structures such as the Marin County Buildings indicate a deterioration of quality and inspiration. But the architect's final period also gave birth to at least one of his most famous structures – New York's Guggenheim Museum – as well as other buildings that seem to point far into the architectural future.

Wright's late buildings are often based on shapes and forms that were unusual and new to the architect. The great spirals of the Guggenheim and the Morris Gift Shop, the circular dome of the Marin County Buildings and the arc shape of the Second Jacobs House are all examples of this. Although Wright continued to produce buildings with rectangular rooms, he seemed especially preoccupied in his later years with curves and circles.

Some of Wright's later work was much more closely based on concepts that he had pioneered years before – for example, combining the Usonian House with concrete-block construction to create what he called the 'Usonian Automatic', a house that clients could build themselves. But Wright also looked forward in more radical ways. His use of a sheltering earth bank and a curving 'hemicycle' of warmth-gathering windows in the Second Jacobs House of 1944 points clearly towards ideas of energy efficiency and sensitivity to nature that are being explored by architects today. As clients and architects recognize more and more the point of minimizing our impact on the earth's resources, Wright's ideas on organic architecture take on a new urgency and importance.

THE
LATER
WORKS

Second Jacobs House

The second house that Wright designed for journalist Herbert Jacobs and his wife Katherine is a much more important design than its small size suggests. Two key features of the building are a curving wall of glass oriented towards the sun and a protective earth bank, or berm, sheltering the house from the cold northerly winds. Both of these features prefigure the experiments of architects today as they try out ways of working with nature to conserve energy and create a nurturing domestic environment.

Location
Middleton, Wisconsin

Client
Herbert and Katherine Jacobs

Date
1944

Main material
Stone, earth, wood

Herbert Jacobs and his wife liked their first Wright house in Madison, Wisconsin (see pages 106–107), but about half a dozen years after it was built, the city began to expand around it and the Jacobs decided to move away from the urban sprawl. Once more they turned to Wright and once more he produced an innovative design – a house planned in the shape of an arc, sheltered from the winds on the north side by a bank of earth.

Working with earth and sun Wright was convinced that this earth-sheltered design, the first of its kind, was an important new departure, and was determined to get it built. He wrote to Jacobs, '… if you don't get what is on the boards some other fellow will. So watch out. It's good. I think we have a real "first" that you will like a lot.' The architect was convinced that his idea would work because it was a building at one with the solar cycle. The curving front of the house would be tracked by the sun's path, bringing its warmth into the house and turning the circular garden in front of the building into a suntrap. Wright called the design a 'solar hemicycle', referring to the semi-circular design on which it is based, although the house itself occupies only 120 degrees – the 30 degrees on either side are filled with planting, to make the complete semi-circle.

OPPOSITE This photograph of the interior shows clearly how the upper rooms are on a wooden mezzanine that forms the living-room ceiling, and how the large windows bring warmth and light to both lower and upper levels. The pool in the living-room floor acts as an unusual link between indoors and outdoors.

The plan is quite simply laid out on one main floor with a mezzanine above suspended from the roof on metal rods in order to keep the main floor clear of pillars. The first floor consists of one large curving room, the living room, which includes a kitchen area at one end. Three smaller circles break into the windowless rear wall – one is a stone hearth, another a round stone tower for utilities that also contains the staircase. The third circle is a pool, which lies half inside the living room and half outside on the terrace. Its presence reminds us how Wright liked to bring all the fundamental 'elements' – fire, air, earth and water – into his houses. The bedrooms are above on the mezzanine floor, sharing the living room's large south-facing windows. The long row of windows and glazed doors look out over a sunken garden.

A house without walls
Because one long side is earth-sheltered and one glazed, the house has few conventional outside walls, just a core of limestone at either end. The roof is flat, and overhangs the glazed front of the house, so that the building is shaded from the strong summer sun. The entrance is unconventional too. Wright drove an entrance passage through the berm, giving the impression of entering a stone-lined cave. This unusual entry makes the berm feel more part of the house and heightens the impression of the house emerging from the earth bank beside it. It also affords the house an extra touch of drama as well as providing the sense of entering a light space through a shaded entry, an effect that Wright employed in many of his houses.

This design was revolutionary. By sinking the house into the earth in the way he did, Wright protected it from the bitter north and northwesterly winds, increasing comfort and reducing heating costs. The heating was also supplemented by the sunshine through the glazed wall, and an earth-sheltered house retains the heat well, so once it has been warmed up in the winter, it does not need much extra heat to keep it warm – and it also stays cool in the summer. And if they did get too hot, the Jacobs family had their pool to cool off in.

The Jacobs's second house took a long time to build. The family moved to the farm on the site in 1942 and Wright produced the plans for the new house in 1944. But by then the USA had entered the Second World War, and materials and labour were short. Wright had designed the house to be built with the simplest materials – wooden posts and beams, local earth, and stone. With the exception of the stone, most of these materials were easy to handle, so the Jacobses did much of the construction work themselves. They enlisted the help of some local farm workers to do the stonework. These men were Swiss immigrants and they laid the stone in the way they had learned in Europe. This caused a dispute between Wright and his client when the architect heard that the stonework had been badly laid. This was not actually true, and when Wright saw the result he was reconciled with Jacobs and sent a bulldozer and driver to shape the earth berm to the correct 45-degree angle. It took until 1949 to get the house finished.

BELOW The south-facing windows of the house are sheltered by the hidden earth bank behind, and the lawn in front of the building is also protected from the breeze. This makes both the house and the garden a suntrap – both a pleasant place to relax and a gathering point for solar energy to keep the house itself warm.

Shorewood Hills Unitarian Church

The Unitarian Church at Shorewood Hills is one of Frank Lloyd Wright's most successful public buildings. Its main auditorium and 'hearth room' are based on two triangles coming together to make a large, diamond-shaped space. This space is lit by a large, clear-glass window and covered by a sweeping pitched roof, which points towards the heavens. The church triumphantly succeeds in using space to give an atmosphere of uplift.

Location
Shorewood Hills,
Madison, Wisconsin
Client
Unitarian congregation
of Shorewood Hills
Date
1947
Main material
Stone, concrete, copper

Wright's ancestors included founding members of the Unitarian Church and as a young man he had worshipped at the Unitarian Unity Temple in Oak Park, a building he redesigned after a fire (see pages 32–35). Unity Temple was one of the great buildings of the architect's early career, a structure in which he rethought what it meant to build a church. It used a 'modern' material – poured concrete – to create forms and spaces unlike those of any previous place of worship. Towards the end of his life, Wright was given the opportunity to design another Unitarian church, in a place close to his heart – the suburb of Shorewood Hills in Madison, Wisconsin.

The sweeping roof
Once again, as he had done in the Unity Temple, Wright chose to create a strong outer form for the building to enclose an equally striking interior space. This time, the form came from the roof. This is a pitched construction that soars from a level quite near the ground, climbing to a high peak or 'prow' that shelters a tall, clear-glass window behind the pulpit, the focal point of the interior. The roof, culminating at this peak above the window, eliminates the need for a spire – it is already sufficiently high and skyward-pointing to lift the worshipper's eye to the heavens.

The roof is clad in copper, which is joined along pronounced ridges that follow the roof line and emphasize its shape. Wright compared the resulting 'folded' form of the pitched roof to a pair of hands held together in prayer. This description is almost certainly a rationalization after the event, and some writers attribute it to Wright's wife Olgivanna rather than to the architect himself. The upward-looking form is symbolic enough without this additional metaphor.

Wright had another idea about the great 'prow' of the church, one that did not work as well as he had planned. This was to use the exterior overhang of the roof to shelter a single large bell. As church towers and steeples often house bells, this was another way of proving that the roof overcame the need for a tower or spire. But this notion backfired. The bell was duly hung, but when the wind got up it swung violently, threatening to shatter the glass window behind it. The offending object was quietly removed.

Interior spaces
The main interior space is divided in two by a break in the roof line. The larger part is the auditorium, where services are held. A congregation of some 250 people can sit here – Wright designed benches for them, which can be moved if events call for a different seating configuration. Behind the auditorium is the other, linked space, known as the hearth room. This was originally separated from the auditorium by a curtain, specially made by the women of the congregation to a design by Wright. This could be pulled aside so that the two spaces could merge, providing extra seating for larger assemblies if required.

The construction work on the church was carried out partly by volunteer labour. Members of the congregation helped to transport tons of stone to the site, and members of the Taliesin Fellowship worked on site, speeding up progress so that the building could be dedicated in the summer of 1951.

ABOVE Whether or not we accept the metaphor that has been used for the roof of the church, involving hands held clasped in prayer, the structure is clearly successful in giving an impression of uplift, and of pointing towards the sky. The building is also an effective study in textures, with a strong contrast between the rough stone and the smooth underside of the roof.

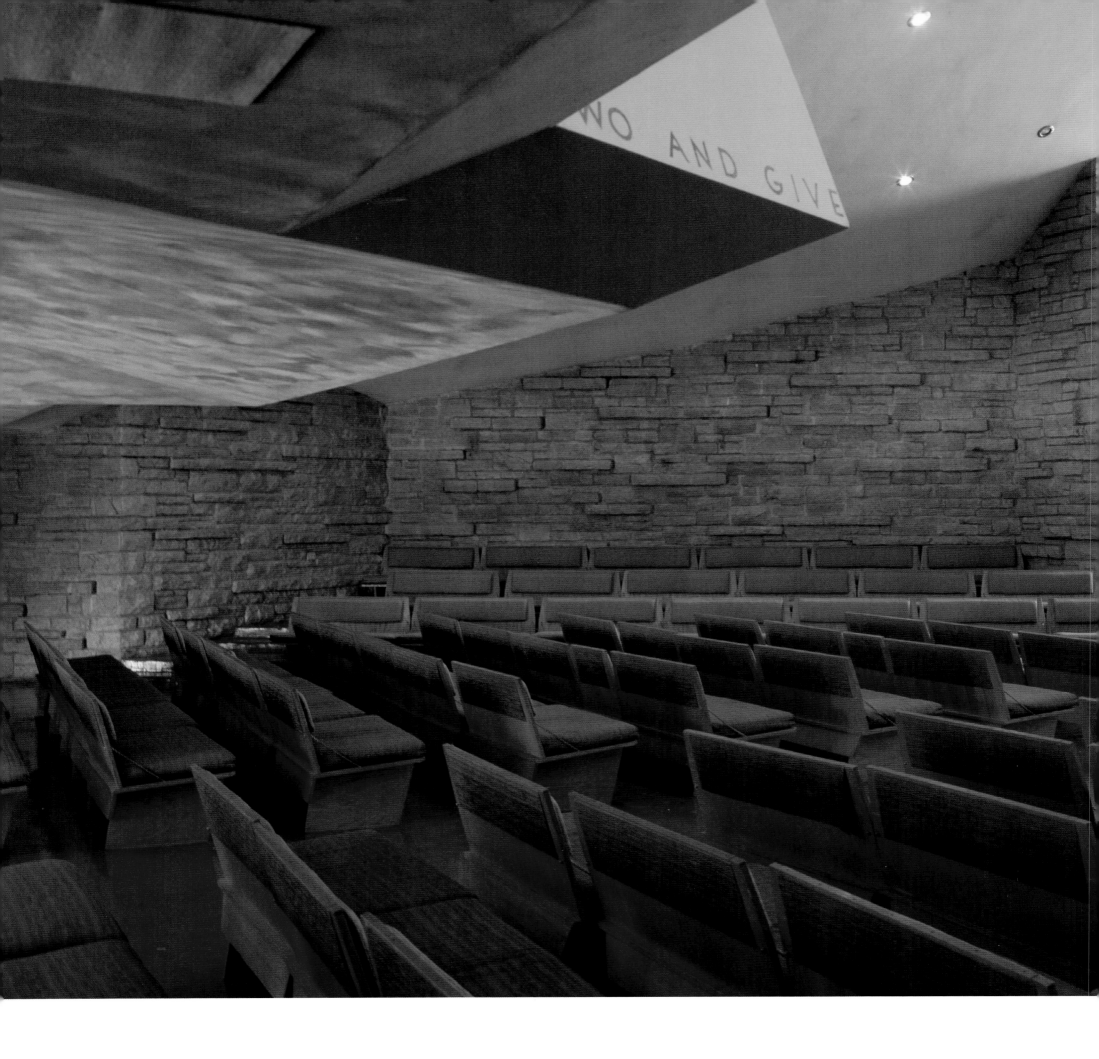

Shorewood Hills Unitarian Church
146

Finishing touches

Among the finishing touches of the interior is an inscription on the face of the low ceiling of the hearth room. This has been variously described as an 'old parable' and as a quotation from an ancient Persian poet. Whatever its source, it was provided by Wright, and might even consist of the words of the architect himself. The unpunctuated wording is as follows: 'DO YOU HAVE A LOAF OF BREAD BREAK THE LOAF IN TWO AND GIVE HALF FOR SOME FLOWERS OF THE NARCISSUS FOR THY BREAD FEEDS THE BODY INDEED BUT THE FLOWERS FEED THE SOUL'.

Later developments

To the west of the main church auditorium extends a loggia gallery, with a series of rooms leading off it. These were originally designed as schoolrooms, with a larger room at the far end called the West Living Room, which was planned to form part of a parsonage. The West Living Room was never used for its intended purpose and the schoolrooms were later converted to office space, when Taliesin Associated Architects built a new education wing beyond. The church itself, however, has survived in its original use, having been given a new copper roof covering in the 1970s, when it was discovered that the original copper had been too thin and was causing structural problems to the timbers beneath it. With these difficulties resolved, the church looks set to have a long life as an unusual and inspiring place of worship.

LEFT The distinction between textured stone and plain white ceiling is also used in the interior. But the dominant impression here is one of light, which floods through the big window and is reflected off the pale surfaces to striking effect.

BELOW The plan of the church is dominated by the main auditorium with its adjoining hearth room. On either side are two asymmetrical wings. One contains the entrance and lobby, with office accommodation neatly tucked in next to the lobby. The other, longer wing was mainly made up of a row of classrooms, which were later converted to offices.

KEY
1 ENTRY
2 LOBBY
3 HEARTH ROOM
4 AUDITORIUM
5 KITCHEN
6 STUDY
7 OFFICE
8 SCHOOL ROOMS
9 LOGGIA/GALLERY
10 WEST LIVING ROOM
11 TOILETS

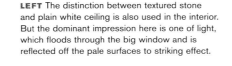

Morris Gift Shop

The Morris Gift Shop is unlike any other shop in the world. Instead of the usual large plate-glass window, Wright designed a solid wall of brickwork with a large entrance – there is no display window at all. Inside, the interior features a big spiral ramp and carefully designed lighting above a large central space. By rethinking traditional store architecture in this way, Wright gave shoppers a new experience, one in which architectural quality is intended to complement the quality of the goods inside.

Location
San Francisco, California

Client
V.C. Morris

Date
1948

Main material
Brick, reinforced concrete

OPPOSITE Instead of a conventional shop window, the store presents to the street a tall blank wall built of brickwork of the highest quality. The doorway, with its beautiful brick arch, catches the eye and offers a tantalizing glimpse of the illuminated interior, tempting passing shoppers to enter.

BELOW The gift shop's internal ramp embraces the lower floor, gracefully sweeping its way towards the upper level. Although some have perceived the ramp's spiral geometry as a kind of rehearsal for the Guggenheim Museum, it works in the opposite way to the ramp at the Guggenheim, directing customers' eyes inwards towards the lower sales floor, rather than out towards the walls as in the museum.

Shops usually offer limited opportunities for an architect. Most retailers want a big window at the front and plenty of well-lit space inside. They are not interested in strong architectural design, which may distract shoppers from the products on display, and are likely to change elements such as signs and lighting quite often as corporate identities get revamped. A whole industry of shopfitting has evolved to facilitate these changes, and this is not an area in which there is much scope for the architect who wants his or her work to survive.

Rethinking retail So when V.C. Morris came to Wright to design a new gift shop in San Francisco, the architect might have backed off, designed a plate-glass frontage, and left it at that. Not Frank Lloyd Wright. The shop for Morris is one of the best examples of Wright's lateral thinking. Turning the problem upside-down, Wright proposed not a big window, but a solid brick wall, a façade of high quality brickwork relieved only by some lights and a magnificent entrance consisting of a sweeping arch made up of four stepped concentric courses of brick.

Inside, the building is just as remarkable. True enough, there is a generous floor area where Morris could display his stock, which consisted of glasswares and ceramics together with items in silver and gold. But there is also the most dramatic touch – a great spiral ramp running around and upward, leading to an upper display area and turning the square showroom into a circle.

A new design logic When Morris saw the design, he was worried. Where were the windows? How were shoppers going to know what he had for sale? Not surprisingly, Wright was prepared with an answer: 'We are not going to dump your beautiful merchandise on the street, but create an arch-tunnel of glass into which the passers-by may look and be enticed. As they penetrate further into the entrance, seeing the shop inside with its spiral ramp and tables set with fine china and crystal, they will suddenly push open the door, and you've got them!'

This was shrewd thinking, and Wright knew it. People who window-shop will not usually come in and buy anything, but once they enter the shop, they are much more likely to make a purchase. By creating the most tempting entrance on the street, Wright was encouraging more people to come into the shop. And everything about the building – the big blank wall, the recessed entrance defined by its courses of bricks, the well-lit interior within, the glimpse of the spiral ramp, just visible through the entrance – all these elements draw in the passer-by.

Wright was defying traditional retail thinking, but Morris saw the new logic he had created, and gave Wright the go-ahead. The result lived up to its promise. While the exterior was dark and mysterious, the architect flooded the interior with light from a series of translucent globe-shaped fittings in the ceiling. The gold, silver and crystal on the tables and in their display cases caught the light, and people were indeed drawn in through the tempting doorway to the glittering interior. It is easy to see the parallels between the Morris Shop and the Guggenheim Museum, which has a still bigger spiral ramp and which Wright was designing at the same time. But both show that Wright, towards the end of his career, still had the ability to think a building through from first principles, and come up with something new.

ABOVE The ramp and the interior walls are beautifully finished, their smooth, pale surfaces highlighted by the polished brass handrail and the round and semi-circular openings in the walls. Wright's aim was to keep the design simple, to avoid distracting the customer from the all-important goods on sale.

Carlson House

With its striking use of colour and unusual materials, the Raymond Carlson House in Phoenix, Arizona, is very different from any other Wright house. It is constructed of flat panels of an off-white material called transite, which contrast happily with the blue-painted timber framework. The architect chose the material because it provided a new way of building cheaply. It also inspired him to create an ingeniously planned house with a range of comfortable social and private spaces.

Location
Phoenix, Arizona
Client
Raymond Carlson
Date
1950
Main material
Wood, transite panels

Raymond Carlson was a friend of Frank Lloyd Wright, one of several in the architect's circle who were journalists. Carlson was the editor of the magazine *Arizona Highways*, and the men met when Carlson approached Wright to ask him for an article in 1940. The editor published several pieces about Wright and the two became close, Carlson and his wife going to dinner parties at Taliesin West. So when Carlson wanted to build a house, it was natural that he should approach Wright – although he did so with a warning that he was on a strict budget.

Working with transite Wright responded enthusiastically. He had in mind a simple, cheap construction technique that would save money and be simple to build. He designed the house on a 4-foot (1.2-m) grid, creating a framework of 4-inch x 4-inch (10-cm x 10-cm) timber uprights, each 4 feet (1.2 m) apart. For the infill between the posts, he used transite. This was a substance consisting of a core of sugar-cane-fibre insulating board covered on either side with sheeting made up of a mix of asbestos and cement. The material was strong, waterproof, fire-resistant, and cheap. It also came in convenient 4-foot (1.2-m) wide panels.

OPPOSITE A view of the northern façade shows the glazed front of the living room, with the taller tower-like structure, containing the bedrooms and Carlson's penthouse study, to the left. Much of the area of the living room accommodates a roof garden, bounded by a low balustrade made of a blue-and-white framework, like the rest of the house.

ABOVE One end of the Carlson House shows the simple effect created by the pale transite material used for the walls and by the blue-painted framework. Around the base of the structure an open area allows light to enter the windows of the kitchen and dining area, which are located in a semi-basement.

Carlson House
152

The construction of wooden posts and transite panels was so easy to build that the Carlsons did much of the construction themselves, to keep the cost down. Wright admired their hard work – not just because they showed their willingness to get their hands dirty but also because of their commitment to the house. Their work convinced Wright that their budget really was limited, and in the end he waived his architect's fee.

Wright specified that the timber uprights should be painted with a pale-blue enamel paint. This makes a strong contrast with the off-white transite boards between and has the practical purpose of protecting the wood against the fierce Arizona climate. Wright did not usually like painting wood, and with his honest, natural approach to architecture he rejected hiding one surface with another. He wrote, 'In organic architecture there is little or no room for appliqué of any kind. I have never been fond of paints or of wallpaper or anything which must be applied *to* other things as a surface.' But because of the practical considerations he made an exception with this paint surface, and the Carlson House looks unlike most other Wright buildings as a result.

A split-level house

The Carlsons' tight budget also meant that they had to choose a plot that was far from ideal. It was a small corner site, quite close to neighbours' houses, and Wright had to use all his ingenuity to give them the privacy they needed. He achieved this in part by angling the house on the plot, so that it does not face the neighbours directly. But his other solution was more radical, and unusual for Wright. The house is in two parts – a long, low section that houses the living room, and an end tower of three floors containing the other rooms. The floor levels in this end tower are staggered in relation to the ground-level living room. So the lower floor of the tower, containing the kitchen and dining room, is actually half a level below ground; the second floor, where the bedrooms are located, is up a half-level from the living room; and the top floor of the tower, housing Carlson's penthouse study, is a level and a half above the living room. This split-level layout has two important consequences. First, the window levels of these rooms are at different heights to those in the neighbours' houses, increasing privacy. Second, the end tower, although high, is not too high, because part of its lowest floor is sunk below ground level.

A range of rooms

As usual in his Usonian and other 'middle-income' houses, the living room of the Carlson House is by far the largest room – and the effective space is made still greater because it opens on to a terrace. The other rooms are quite small – the dining space is fitted in next to the kitchen and separated from it by a bar; the bedrooms are compact. But Wright made best use of the available space by including plenty of built-in closets. He also gave his friend a special indulgence – the generously proportioned penthouse study, on its own at the top of the tower and opening on to a roof garden covering most of the living-room roof. This was a dual-purpose space, a place where Carlson could work on his own, or where he could invite friends for a drink or a barbecue on the roof.

The Carlson House lasted well, but in the 1970s had to be sold when Carlson went into a nursing home. By then the house was looking old and uncared-for. However, a sympathetic restoration was undertaken under Charles Schiffner, an architect who had been an apprentice at Taliesin, and the house now looks as good as new.

LEFT Inside the living room the pattern of naturally finished wall uprights and ceiling beams reflects the fact that the house is laid out on a 4-foot (1.2-m) grid. Fitted seating is attached to one long and one short wall. Part of the low stone surround of the fireplace is just visible on the extreme left of the picture.

BELOW A simple plan based on a 4-foot (1.2-m) grid with no long wings helped to make the Carlson House straightforward to build. A terrace was provided at ground level in addition to the roof garden immediately above the living room.

KEY
1. ENTRY
2. LIVING ROOM
3. BEDROOM
4. MASTER BEDROOM
5. CLOAK
6. BATH
7. CARPORT
8. TERRACE
9. FIREPLACE

4' 0"

Plan of second level

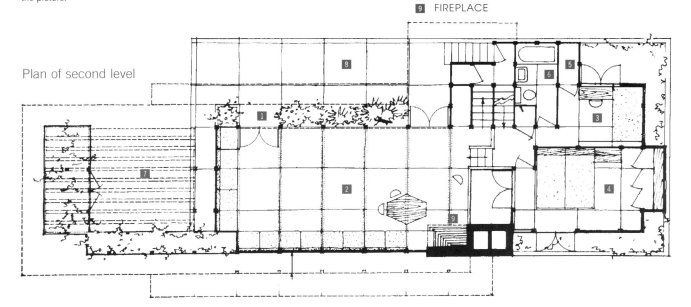

Price Company Tower

An irregularly shaped and beautifully finished building in Bartlesville, Oklahoma, the Price Company Tower was Frank Lloyd Wright's tallest built structure. In it, he worked out some of his ideas about skyscraper structure and planning, and provided a landmark building for his client. As usual with Wright, the tower shows the architect's hand in every detail, from the specially designed furniture to the abstract mural — its design reflecting the structural geometry of the building — installed in Harold Price's own office.

Location
Bartlesville, Oklahoma
Client
Harold C. Price Sr
Date
1952
Main material
Reinforced concrete

It is ironic that Frank Lloyd Wright, designer of long, low, ground-hugging houses, always wanted to build a tall skyscraper. For years, the closest he got was the 14-floor research tower for the Johnson Wax Company (see page 115); but throughout his life he planned various tall structures that remained unbuilt, culminating in a notorious proposal for a mile-high skyscraper in Chicago. So when company owner Harold C. Price approached Wright for a new headquarters building, Wright persuaded his new client to consider a tower.

Reviving an old design As it happened, the architect had in mind an old design for an apartment tower for St Mark's-in-the-Bouwerie, New York. Wright had drawn up the New York design in 1929, but because of the Great Depression the project had never come to fruition. Its structure was based on a central reinforced-concrete core containing stairs and elevators, from which the concrete floor slabs were cantilevered out. In other words it was like a tree, with the core acting as the trunk and the floor slabs as branches. The other unusual feature of the New York tower was that its floor plan had a complex geometry combining a cross-shaped element with various rectangles, giving a tower of irregular but satisfying shape.

When he had convinced Price that a tower was a good idea for his headquarters building, Wright developed a version of his New York tower for Price's site in Bartlesville, Oklahoma. He retained the tree-like structure and based the plan on a square superimposed on a pinwheel, so that the building looks from the outside like a square tower with polygonal ridges sticking out of the sides. The resulting exterior looks more elegant and more 'right' than it sounds.

The tower is actually not very much taller than the earlier tower Wright had built for Johnson — it is 221 feet (67 m) tall and contains 19 floors, of which two comprise

LEFT This office interior shows how the tower's unusual shape allows even many of the smaller rooms to have windows facing in more than one direction. The furniture is specially designed both to make efficient use of the available space and to mirror the tower's irregular angles.

the base of the tower and 17 make up the main vertical mass of the building. There is also a radio antenna spire, giving extra height. From the outside, the tower looks impressive thanks to high-quality finishes that include copper fascia panels, copper louvres and gold-tinted glass.

The interiors and furniture All this height

gave the tower much more accommodation than Price needed for his offices, so Wright designed parts of the building as apartments, parts as offices for rent, and parts as office space for Price's company. The apartments are double height, with living room and kitchen on one level, bedrooms on the other, and private interconnecting stairs. Price's own office was at the very top of the tower, and opened on to a roof garden.

Because of the unusual floor plan, most of the rooms in the tower are very irregular in shape. So Wright designed a range of furniture for the building – some of it built-in, some of it free-standing – to fit into the unusual spaces. It worked well, and, as well as housing Price's offices, the building became an office base for a variety of professionals including physicians, dentists, lawyers and accountants. The architect Bruce Goff rented an office in the tower and also moved into one of the apartments.

The Price Company stayed in the tower until 1981, when they sold the building to Phillips Petroleum, who kept it for 20 years. In the year 2000 they gave the building to the Price Tower Arts Center, and it now houses a museum of art and design, a hotel (the Inn at Price Tower), a restaurant and various other tenants. The rich and varied life of this unusual mixed-used tower continues.

LEFT With its striped sides and series of odd-shaped projections, the Price Tower is one of America's most irregularly shaped skyscrapers. However, the bizarre shape has a clear planning logic, with the projections housing such facilities as emergency stairs and the kitchens of the apartments.

Price House

This house for businessman Harold Price gets its unusual appearance from Wright's attempt to create a building that would be at home in the Arizona desert. Its 'inverted' concrete-block piers, with flat roofs apparently hovering just above them, give the building a strong outline in the desert sun, while its beautifully conceived central atrium, partly open to the elements, is a very special and inviting way of bringing the house and the surrounding landscape together.

Location
Paradise Valley, Arizona

Client
Harold C. and
Mary Lou Price

Date
1954

Main material
Concrete blocks, steel

The idea of a desert house meant several things to Frank Lloyd Wright – finding an appropriate material for the dry, harsh terrain; casting jagged shadows that were right in a place of strong light and craggy rocks; opening up the building to give ventilation while also providing a way to shut out the cold. All these requirements are answered in the house the architect designed for Harold Price, for whose company he had built the Price Tower (see pages 154–155) two years previously.

Building at speed Price wanted a summer house in the desert where he and his wife could entertain their grandchildren, so they needed plenty of bedrooms, a place for the children to play, and a pool. They also wanted their house quickly – ideally within eight months of the start of the build. Wright moved decisively – he was well disposed to Price because the businessman had already given him a rare opportunity to build a skyscraper – and came up with a construction method that would allow the work to be done at speed. The house was to have seven bedrooms and a footprint of some 5,000 square feet (465 sq m), so the builders needed all the speed they could muster. It helped that Wright was on hand for frequent site visits – his base at Taliesin West was around 10 miles (16 km) away.

Wright used a concrete-block construction for large parts of the structure. The blocks appear both as ordinary walls and as extra-ordinary piers that splay out from narrow bases to broader tops, ending just below the roof. Out of the tops of these piers come thin tubes of steel that hold up the roof. The effect is that the roof 'floats' just above the massive piers, a magical effect and one that allows the piers to produce the strong, jagged outlines that Wright wanted for this desert house.

The central atrium These tapering piers dominate the large living room and are used in smaller rooms in the house, such as the bedrooms. They also surround what is in some ways the most striking and original part of the house, the atrium that connects the living room with the bedroom wing. The atrium is a part-indoor, part-outdoor space that brings the house and desert together. It is covered with a ceiling, but this is pierced with a large square skylight to give the occupants the best of both worlds – some natural sunlight but also shade from the desert heat. The gaps between the piers can be left open to admit the breeze, or closed off with artfully designed shutters when it gets cold.

At the centre of the atrium, beneath the skylight, is a fountain with a circular basin to catch any rain that falls through the skylight. In one corner is a fireplace to give extra warmth when the desert temperature falls. So within this imposing atrium space, three of the traditional 'elements' – air, water and fire – are admitted. Anyone in the atrium can look out at the fourth element – earth – in the form of the surrounding desert, and the presence of the four elements creates the kind of harmony that Wright relished.

Furnishings and finishes Although built of concrete and steel, and although it fits well into the harsh desert landscape, the Price House is not cold and uninviting. The use of warm red concrete floors, mahogany shutters (many decorated in rich metallic tones), brass light fittings and mahogany furniture produces an effect of great warmth and richness. And the floating roof gives the place a kind of magic that only a master architect could conjure. Seldom has the desert seemed so inviting.

OPPOSITE Red steps lead past the guest wing of the Price House, up to an atrium, and towards the block containing the living and dining rooms beyond. This varied collection of spaces is unified by the grey concrete-block walls, the steel poles and the flat roofs with their pierced edging.

Beth Sholom Synagogue

Wright designed his only synagogue at the end of his life, while he was also busy with his work on the Guggenheim Museum. Like the more famous Guggenheim, the Beth Sholom Synagogue is a building with a remarkably strong form, likened to a glowing mountain of light, which expresses a unique interior. To create it, Wright had to learn a new vocabulary of symbolism and ritual, and, doing so in collaboration with an especially sympathetic client, designed one of his most successful buildings.

Location
Elkins Park, Philadelphia

Client
The Board of Directors of the Congregation of Beth Sholom

Date
1954

Main material
Concrete, steel, glass, fibreglass

The congregation of Beth Sholom in Philadelphia built their first synagogue in 1922. The congregation grew and also prospered, many families choosing to move to the suburbs. By the 1950s, it seemed right to them and to their rabbi, Mortimer J. Cohen, to move their synagogue to the suburbs, too. They bought some land in Elkins Park, building a school and community centre and beginning to raise money for a synagogue. When Rabbi Cohen discussed the proposal with his friend Boris Blai, Dean of the Tyler Art School of Temple University, Philadelphia, Blai recommended his friend Frank Lloyd Wright as architect.

Rabbi and architect
When Cohen approached Wright by letter, the rabbi enclosed some rough sketches of how he thought the new synagogue should be planned. Normally Wright would have bridled at a prospective client trying to dictate a design in this way, but this time the architect took on the job, perhaps respecting the rabbi's deep thought and sincerity about what he wanted. Although the design evolved over the months and then years, Wright retained many of Cohen's suggestions. Uniquely, he took so much from Cohen that he later went on record as saying that the rabbi should be credited as joint architect.

Rabbi Cohen did not simply put the architect right about details of synagogue design that he might not know (that the Ark should be raised above the main floor by at least three steps, for example); he also made some comments that had a profound impact on Wright. One of these was the notion that the synagogue should reflect both the Jewish experience and American culture. The form of the building is clearly inspired by this idea. Tied to the ground by low walls of concrete, the building is dominated by the tall, tent-like structure of metal, glass and plastic that towers above these walls. After the drafting room at Taliesin West (see pages 120–123), this is the most tent-like of all Wright's buildings, and it recalls both Native North American tepees and the concept of the tabernacle as a tent-like shrine. The structure is also shaped like a mountain, alluding to another of Rabbi Cohen's metaphors, that of the tabernacle as a 'travelling Mount Sinai'. It is a richly symbolic building, without drawing on any of the old-fashioned architectural styles, from Romanesque to neo-Georgian, that architects had previously used when building synagogues.

A memorable structure
This great translucent mountain is achieved with an ingenious structure. The building is an irregular hexagon, and from three of its corners a large steel

BELOW The structures along the ridges of the roof are stylized menorot (seven-branched candelabra), which form one of the central symbols of Judaism. One of the key symbols of the tabernacle and used in the Temple in Jerusalem, the menorah is also a symbol of Israel. The menorot on the roof of the Beth Sholom Synagogue can be seen from every direction.

ABOVE Throughout history, places of worship have been built in the shape of mountains, as if reaching towards the heavens, but rarely has the effect been as clear as in the Beth Sholom Synagogue. The pale structure recalls Mount Sinai, and during both night and day resembles a mountain of light.

tripod frame stretches to the top of the roof. Each beam is 117 feet (36 m) in length and the framework supports a double-layer roof covering consisting of white corrugated wired glass outside and reinforced pale corrugated fibreglass inside, with an air gap between the two layers to provide insulation. As well as illuminating the main hall with gentle natural light during the daytime, the roof glows with artificial light at night. Light is nearly always richly symbolic in religious buildings, and Judaism, with its notions of the Torah as 'light', is no exception.

The synagogue is also, of course, a good example of Wright working against his principle that a building should be of its landscape rather than on it. Its great towering structure could not be 'of' the land on which it stands, for all the power of the concrete walls to tie land and building together. But the synagogue is very much 'of' its religious environment. It may be like no other synagogue, but it captures

well the essence of what such a building should be, an embodiment of the light of the Torah, and indeed, a house of peace.

Experiencing the interior
From the outside, the form of the building is clear; however, typically with a Wright building, the visitor does not experience the great hall of the synagogue immediately on entering. The lower floor contains the smaller Sisterhood Chapel, together with a pair of lounges. To reach the great hall, you must climb one of a pair of ramps or stairs from the lower level. Arriving via one of the ramps from the vestibule, you climb to a corner of the building near the base of one of the legs of the tripod frame, which leads the eye upward to the great roof before you look down to see the array of seating; the central bimah; and the Ark, containing the Torah scrolls, beyond. It is a dramatic interior to enter in this way, but also one in which there is an atmosphere of reverence and faith. Of all Wright's religious buildings it is the one, for most visitors, that best embodies a sense of the spiritual – of architect, religious leader and congregation working together for one end.

ABOVE The stained-glass shade of the chandelier is decorated in symbolic colours – blue for wisdom; green for understanding; gold for beauty; red for strength, courage and justice; white for mercy – which are also used in the mantles that cover the synagogue's Torah scrolls.

OPPOSITE The seats are arranged around the central Ark, in which the Torah scrolls are kept. Above the Ark is a shining ornament made of aluminium and glass. This design refers to the words of the prophet Isaiah, who describes God surrounded by seraphim and cherubim – dazzling creatures, each with six wings.

RIGHT The plan of the main floor of the synagogue shows how Wright took advantage of the building's unusual geometry. The structure is an irregular but symmetrical hexagon, and this shape allows for the seats to be arranged in three blocks, each angled towards the central Ark.

KEY
1. CANOPY OVER ENTRANCE
2. UPPER PART OF VESTIBULE
3. MEMORIAL TABLET
4. RAMP DOWN TO VESTIBULE
5. CANTOR
6. RABBI
7. CANTOR'S STUDY
8. RABBI'S STUDY
9. ARK

Plan of upper (temple) level

Toufic Kalil House

Wright's house for Dr Toufic H. Kalil and his wife Mildred is an early example of a new kind of building that Wright designed to be simple and cheap to construct. The structure was based on concrete blocks, but Wright took their manufacture and use a stage further than in his concrete houses of the 1920s, not just in economy of means, but also in the creative way in which glazed blocks were used to bring natural light into the rooms.

Location
Manchester, New Hampshire

Client
Toufic H. and Mildred Kalil

Date
1955

Main material
Concrete blocks

At the end of his life, Wright was still worrying away at a problem that had always occupied him: how can a person on a really limited budget have an architect-designed home with 'the liberation, the sense of freedom that comes with true architecture'? Even the Usonian Houses that he had built for clients in the late 1930s had come at a price that stretched the resources of a college lecturer. Was it possible to reduce the cost still further? Wright decided that it was, and that the way forward was to reduce labour costs by creating a system of construction so simple that the clients could do much of the building work themselves. Enter the kind of house that Wright called the 'Usonian Automatic'.

The concrete structure
For this type of house Wright returned to the concrete-block construction that he had used back in the 1920s in such buildings as La Miniatura (see pages 86–87). The concrete blocks could be cast on site, by ramming concrete into wooden or metal forms. Although there were several different sizes and shapes of block, typical blocks were 2 feet x 1 foot (60 cm x 30 cm), with hollowed-out backs for lightness. The concrete was put into the forms under pressure, so that it set rapidly, meaning that the blocks could be made at speed. As in the 1920s houses, the blocks were grooved around the edges so that they could be 'woven' together with steel rods, before semi-liquid cement was poured into the remaining space to stick them together. Blocks could also be used to construct ceilings, and there were even blocks that were glazed, to create windows.

One of the first of these Usonian Automatics was built for Dr Toufic Kalil and his wife Mildred at Manchester, New Hampshire. As pioneers of the system, they agreed to buy the machine to make the blocks, selling it on to the next client when the block-making was completed. This job took place over winter, so that the house could be built the following summer.

RIGHT The living room is dominated by its wall of pierced blocks, which look out over a terrace accessed through a door in the left-hand wall of the room. The generous height makes the room feel spacious and avoids any impression of heaviness that the ceiling blocks might have caused had they been lower.

ABOVE Sometimes a house made of cast concrete blocks can stand out from its surroundings, its decoration creating bold shadows and strong shapes. But here, the house – backed up against a stand of trees and surrounded by planting – seems to blend into its environment in a way that looks forward to more recent 'low-impact' buildings.

Light and space

What emerged was a house on an L-shaped plan, with one wing containing the carport; one wing the bedrooms; and the central linking block housing the living room, dining area, kitchen and utilities. The most remarkable space is the living room, where one and a half walls consist mainly of blocks with their concrete centres replaced with glass. This not only gives a lavish area of glazing, but also creates a rich pattern of light and shade because the block edges are much thicker and deeper than normal window frames. So the room – which faces southeast, with a south-facing corner – is very light, but glare is reduced by the shadows.

The pattern of concrete and glass also makes a strong impression outside, where the large expanse of glazing to the living room is repeated in smaller sections that light the kitchen, bathroom and bedrooms. This is one way in which the walls of the house, which could be rather forbidding with their concrete surfaces, are broken up and given character and texture.

The Toufic Kalil House beautifully realizes Wright's ability to make warm, inviting forms and spaces out of concrete, a material widely regarded in the 1950s and later as cheap and 'low-status'. Although many of the clients who tried the architect's 'simple' form of construction did not find it as 'automatic' as he had hoped, buildings like this one showed that, if they persevered, they got a house that was liveable, economical and unmistakeably by Frank Lloyd Wright.

Annunciation Greek Orthodox Church

Frank Lloyd Wright's only Greek Orthodox church has a radical structure based on a cross and a circle, two of the faith's most powerful symbols. The result is a building that expresses its purpose perfectly, as well as providing practical accommodation for a range of activities from administration to Sunday school. Although it looks like an extraordinary sculpture in concrete, the building also embodies powerful symbols and has served its congregation well.

Location
Milwaukee, Wisconsin

Client
The congregation of the Annunciation Greek Orthodox Church

Date
1956

Main material
Reinforced concrete

When the Orthodox community of Milwaukee formed a building committee for a new church, they interviewed a number of architects about their plans, but did not at first think of Frank Lloyd Wright. After several interviews, the process seemed to be moving towards a traditional church in the Byzantine style, the kind of design familiar throughout Greece and in other Orthodox churches around the world. Then a committee member reminded them that the most famous architect in the USA lived in Wisconsin: shouldn't they interview him, too? And so it was that Wright got the job — and one last chance to build a place of worship.

Symbol and structure Orthodox Christianity is an ancient branch of the religion and is rich in symbolism and traditions. Among these symbols are the Greek cross, with its equal-length arms. Many Orthodox churches are also roofed with a dome. Wright built both these ideas into the structure of the

OPPOSITE The church is an essay in curves, most of which form a segment of a circle – for example, the great upturned dish of the dome, the segmental windows and the sweeping curve just above ground level. Closer to, more curves reveal themselves – even the planters at each corner are round, echoing the shape of the dome.

BELOW The underside of the edge of the dome is detailed with a series of fins with semi-circles between them. The thin edge of the rim is decorated with hundreds of tiny half-circle motifs. The whole construction casts complex shadows on the adjoining wall.

Annunciation Church. The lower part of the structure is in the shape of a large Greek cross and the roof is a shallow concrete dome. This combination of forms, expressed in pale concrete, gives the building its strong character and also dictates many details of its plan, structure and decoration.

The dome covers the whole of the main building and is some 70 feet (21.3 m) in diameter. Given the extremes of temperature in this part of North America, such a structure will expand and contract a certain amount over the course of a year; so to allow for this, Wright placed the dome on thousands of ball bearings, which rest in a set of steel rails in a reinforced-concrete truss. The truss, which is pierced by curved segmental windows lighting the balcony of the church, itself rests on the four piers that form the ends of the Greek cross.

Inside, there is a large circular balcony beneath the dome, and further seating at entrance level in the arms of the Greek cross and the circular area where cross and dome meet. There is a further level to the building, hidden below ground. This contains a banqueting hall, with service rooms in the arms of the Greek cross, and also a further space, beneath the ground-level garden terrace, containing Sunday-school rooms and offices, some of which open on to a sunken garden. So, although the building is substantial and striking from the outside, it encloses a still larger subterranean space.

Problems and solutions

The dome is an elegant structure, the perfect roof design for the church, but was the cause of problems. Although the ball-bearing system protected the structure from cracks, the materials with which the dome was covered did not prove so durable. Inside, where gold Metalflake had been applied over an asbestos-based insulation, bits of the covering began to come off shortly after construction was finished in 1963. The insulation was replaced with urethane foam. There were similar issues on the outside, which had been covered in blue ceramic mosaic tiles; these had to be replaced with a synthetic resin covering.

Wright did not live to see these problems, or even to watch the Annunciation Church being completed – he died in 1959 and the church was not consecrated until 12 September 1971. But he would have been impressed by the way in which his structure combined with elements such as stained glass, metalwork and icons, to make a space worthy of the deep spiritual beliefs of the congregation.

Solomon R Guggenheim Museum

In the heart of Manhattan, the Solomon R. Guggenheim Museum is a building unlike any other. In this place of skyscrapers and brownstones, of straight avenues and rectangular city blocks, this is a structure based on circles and spirals. Its snail-like exterior and great spiral ramp inside have made it one of the world's most famous museums, and an inspiration to later museum designers who have wanted to create new, unusual and dramatic buildings.

Location
New York, New York State

Client
Solomon R. Guggenheim Foundation

Date
1956

Main material
Reinforced concrete

In 1943 Hilla Rebay, art adviser to Solomon R. Guggenheim, invited Wright to design a new museum to house Guggenheim's collection of modern abstract painting. Some aspects of the proposal put Wright off: he was not a lover of abstract art and the museum was to be in New York, a city that Wright felt was overcrowded and full of undistinguished buildings. But the attractions of a major museum design proved tempting and Wright agreed, embarking on a project that would occupy him for the rest of his life.

A new concept in museum design

Architect and client looked at various sites before settling on one on Fifth Avenue, between 88th and 89th streets. Wright created a museum that, while designed no doubt to surprise and shock, was also based on a big idea. The architect's big design concept turned orthodox museum design upside down, but seemed very logical when it was explained. Most museums are laid out as a series of interconnecting rooms. Visitors wander from one room to another, often retracing their steps as they do so, and frequently getting tired in the process. Why not, Wright reasoned, deliver visitors to the top of the gallery by elevator, and then let them walk slowly down a gently sloping spiral ramp, looking at the art as they go? This way, they avoid 'museum fatigue' and they all walk the same way, so are not constantly retracing their steps and crossing one anothers' paths.

LEFT The concrete walls bear no decoration, no interruption of their pure forms, except for the name of the museum spelled out in widely spaced dark capital letters. The letters snake their way along the curving wall at the corner of the building, leading the eye around its form.

ABOVE Low sunlight warms the pale walls of the Guggenheim Museum, casting shadows of trees and highlighting the texture of the concrete. Even on a dull day the unique rounded forms of the museum bring a special visual richness to this city of rectangular blocks and tall, square buildings; in the sun, the structure pulls off further surprises.

So Wright designed the main part of the museum as a great spiral, larger at the top, tapering slightly so that it is smaller at the bottom, like an upside-down Tower of Babel. A sweeping canopy, also curving but on a different centre, protrudes above the entrance, challenging the rectilinear street corner and welcoming visitors. Wright included another, smaller circular block to one side (originally intended to house apartments for Guggenheim and Rebay, but in a revision of the plan given over to offices and storage space, and later converted to exhibition space for the museum's permanent collection). A third section, a tower, was not built because of budgetary constraints.

The effect of the great spiral on Fifth Avenue is nothing short of amazing. Although the architect took inspiration from natural forms such as nautilus shells, the effect is unlike anything out of nature. The smooth rendered sides, with their interplay of curving and straight walls, still seem alien half a century after the building was completed – and would have seemed even more so if the walls had been painted pink, as they are in one of Wright's drawings of the building. But as the museum stands, it is alien in a refreshing way: this is a building that makes you notice it, and then draws you inside.

The museum interior

The interior is just as dramatic. At the centre of the great spiral, a large atrium allows you to look straight up to the skylight with its elegant pattern of glazing bars. The sides of the ramp wrap around this space and the elevator is expressed by a bulge in the lines of the ramp, forming a break in the sweeping spiral. It is a grand space, a kind of modern reinterpretation of the vast staircases in big public buildings. The paintings themselves are displayed in a series of compartments along the ramp, so the idea of a succession of galleries is interpreted in a new way. Descending the ramp, the visitor can enter each successive space and look at the paintings hung on three walls, or turn towards the fourth side, looking into the great atrium and across to the art on the ramp at the other side.

It was and is a space to enjoy, but some were unsure whether it was an ideal space to enjoy paintings. Some complained that the bold design distracted the viewer from the art, others even going so far as to suggest that Wright, who didn't like the collection, was deliberately trying to trump it with his architecture. And there were technical problems, too – the original idea was to hang the paintings on sloping walls, recalling easels, but this was abandoned in favour of a more conventional presentation.

All this took time to get right, and the project, from selecting the site to finishing the build, went on until after the architect's death. And a recent restoration and extension has carried on the work, adding facilities in the neighbouring new building while restoring some of the features of Wright's structure, such as the skylight, so that the museum is closer to the way he envisaged it. It remains unique, but it has inspired other curators and architects, from Berlin to Bilbao, to build landmark museums that catch the eye and engage the mind.

BELOW The experience of visiting the Guggenheim is quite different from walking around a conventional museum. From any point on the ramp, visitors can look across the central space of the gallery to glimpse the pictures on the opposite side, getting a preview of the works of art they will be able to examine more closely as they descend.

RIGHT From the main floor of the gallery, the spiral ramp circles upwards towards the central skylight, with its delicate pattern of glazing bars. This is one of architecture's great sculptural forms, which Wright justified vigorously on practical grounds as a radical rethinking of how a museum should work.

BELOW This plan of the museum shows the ground level. The visitor arrives via the vestibule, taking in the great gallery and the sweep of the ramp before walking to the elevator on the left to ride to the top of the building. Service rooms are tucked away to the right of the elevator shaft.

KEY

1	ENTRANCE/LOGGIA	8	CAFE
2	VESTIBULE	9	GRAND GALLERY
3	MAIN GALLERY	10	MEZZANINE
4	INFORMATION	11	ENTRANCE TO CAFE
5	ELEVATOR	12	SCULPTURE GARDEN
6	COATROOM	13	MONITOR
7	WORKROOM	14	DRIVEWAY

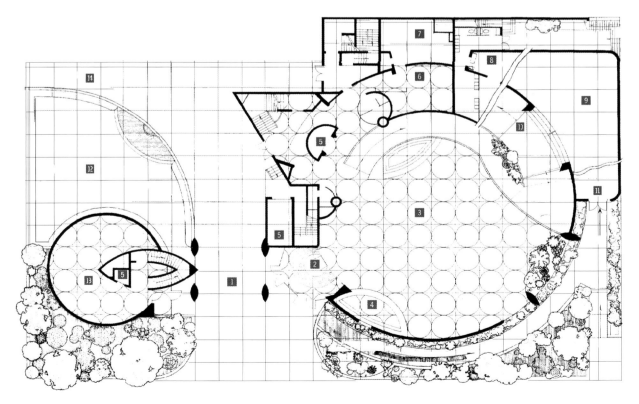

Marin County Buildings

The buildings Wright designed for Marin County, California, are the architect's only government buildings. They show him, at the very end of his life, taking a new direction to come up with a monumental structure stretching across the local hills, articulated with a large dome, a spire, rows of arches, and pale walls. It is an unusual building for Wright, taking rather brash forms and imposing them on a landscape, and, for all its drama, has been taken by some to suggest a falling-off of the architect's powers.

Location
San Rafael, California

Client
The Administration of
Marin County, California

Date
1957

Main material
Reinforced concrete, steel

Wright's Marin Buildings stretch in two long lines between hills, their pale walls standing out from the surrounding trees and water, their tall spire pointing defiantly towards the sky. The two long ranges are connected by a central, dome-topped block, housing a library. In one direction stretches the Administration Building, in the other the Hall of Justice. Both feature rows of arches that make regular holes in their long pale façades, and these arches – the lower ones larger than those nearer the top – have made some writers liken the structure to a great Roman aqueduct, like the famous Pont du Gard that took water to the French city of Nîmes. Inside, long galleried hallways lead to ranges of offices, some with movable walls so that the spaces could be adapted to changing needs. Views out take in the lake, trees and hills of the surrounding country.

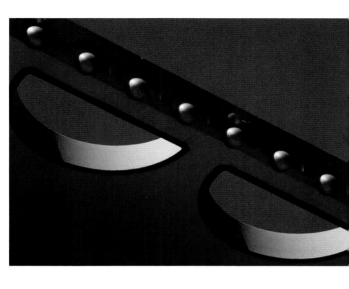

Questions of design

The arches, the big dome and the slender spire are certainly imposing features, signalling a grand building of public importance. But many have found them a little too self-important. It is ironic, for example, that Wright, who spent his life avoiding building churches with spires, should in the end put a spire on a public building – it is actually a ventilation tower, and Wright also meant that it should carry a radio antenna. The arches have been criticized too, partly because, although they look structural, they are not: they are stucco panels on steel frames that are suspended from the concrete floor panels behind them. Although we are used to Wright displaying structural ingenuity, he does not normally come up with this kind of structural dishonesty. A further criticism concerns some of the decoration, including the fascia panels of anodized aluminium and the decorative balls that are widely used, which look somewhat tawdry after Wright's more usual handcrafted materials.

And yet there are things to admire in this, Wright's last large public building. The internal galleries of the Administration Building, their curving fronts reminiscent of the Guggenheim Museum's ramps, tie the interior together. The office space beyond them is flexible and well lit. Even the relationship between building and site is impressive, though the structure is much more imposed on the landscape than is usual in the architect's buildings.

A new direction?

The differences between this late building and Wright's other work has been explained in various ways. Some have pointed to the fact that work on the structure went on long after Wright's death. Other architects from the Taliesin Fellowship continued on the project, and their hand has sometimes been seen in the project as a whole. For others, the differences are to do with the increasing atmosphere of reverence for Wright at Taliesin – no one was allowed to criticize any of his ideas, and every notion, no matter how fanciful, had to be accepted if it came from the lips or the drafting pen of the master. And yet these collaborations and this deference also produced late buildings such as the Beth Sholom Synagogue and the Guggenheim Museum, which are acknowledged as masterpieces.

Perhaps it was simply that Wright, ever wanting to move on, was striving once more for something different. There is still plenty to admire here, and the Marin Buildings attract discussion, debate and the exchange of ideas – something that can be said of every building by Wright, from his early days in Oak Park to his late career as a revered master, designing all over North America.

THE LEGACY OF FRANK LLOYD WRIGHT

THE LEGACY OF FRANK LLOYD WRIGHT is one of the greatest of any architect. It encompasses the buildings that he created and that have survived, many of which are of outstanding quality; the new directions in architecture he pursued, including his concept of organic architecture; and the part he played in creating a uniquely American kind of architecture.

ABOVE In 1958, aged 91, the master architect contemplates one of his drawings. Frank Lloyd Wright kept busy on a number of buildings right up to the end of his life the following year.

Behind all these themes lies one especially strong trait. Wright had an outstanding ability to think an idea through from first principles. He would begin not with some previous model from the remote past, but with the basic requirements of the building and the nature of the site. He thought outwards from these key tenets so that, at their best, his buildings depended less on past styles than on real needs. And so, in theory and often in practice, each building's plan grew from these basic requirements, and the design of the façades, the interiors and even the furnishings derived from them too. This way of thinking a building through inspired later designers and is one example of how Wright's legacy lives on in the way people think about and practise architecture.

The buildings
First and foremost, Frank Lloyd Wright was the architect of some 500 buildings. Around 400 of these still survive, and most of them make a positive contribution both to the places where they are sited and to the lives of the people who use them. Few architects produce so many buildings, or so many of such quality, and they range from factories to hotels, from offices to churches, although the majority are the houses for which he became so famous.

In the face of all this richness and diversity, the American Institute of Architects have selected 17 buildings by Wright that should be retained as examples of his architectural contribution to American culture. These include his most spectacular structures, such as the Johnson Wax Buildings in Racine, Wisconsin, and New York's Guggenheim Museum, as well as some of his most striking houses, like the famous Fallingwater.

Wright's legacy also includes a number of smaller, less well-known buildings that, though less spectacular, have still made a notable contribution to American architecture. These structures include the group of concrete-block houses that Wright designed in California around 1923 and the elegant and economical Usonian Houses, especially those that were created at the end of the 1930s. Large and small, Frank Lloyd Wright's legacy of surviving buildings is one of the most impressive of any architect.

Fellowship and Foundation
Frank Lloyd Wright found a new way of running an architectural practice when he created the Taliesin Fellowship in 1932. Unusually, rather than forming a group of partners and qualified architects, Wright invited those who wanted to learn his kind of

SEVENTEEN KEY BUILDINGS These buildings have been selected by the American Institute of Architects to be retained as examples of Frank Lloyd Wright's architectural contribution to American culture:

Frank Lloyd Wright House and Studio, Oak Park, Illinois
Winslow House, River Forest, Illinois
Unity Temple, Oak Park, Illinois
Willits House, Highland Park, Illinois
Robie House, Chicago, Illinois
Taliesin, Spring Green, Wisconsin
Hollyhock House, Los Angeles, California
Fallingwater, Bear Run, Pennsylvania
Paul and Jean Hanna House, Stanford, California
Johnson Wax Administration Building, Racine, Wisconsin
Johnson Wax Research Tower, Racine, Wisconsin
Taliesin West, Scottsdale, Arizona
Shorewood Hills Unitarian Church, Madison, Wisconsin
Morris Gift Shop, San Francisco, California
Price Company Tower, Bartlesville, Oklahoma
Beth Sholom Synagogue, Elkins Park, Philadelphia
Solomon R Guggenheim Museum, New York, New York State

architecture to join the Taliesin Fellowship as apprentices. They paid to learn and to help Wright run his practice; Wright benefited from a group of enthusiastic and deferential assistants who enabled him to design a large number of buildings. This form of practice did not catch on, but it meant that Wright's ideas on architecture were passed on to many others, producing a long-term influence on American architects. Today, the flame is kept alive by the Taliesin Foundation, which maintains Wright's homes at Taliesin and Taliesin West, and carries out educational work to train architects and to explain Wright's ideas and his legacy.

An American architecture
Frank Lloyd Wright transformed American architecture. In the late 19th century, when he began to practise, the architecture of the USA was already changing. Many buildings were still built in imitation of European styles – there were churches in the Gothic revival or 'pointed' style, industrial buildings in the round-arched Romanesque, and all manner of structures inspired by the classical Second Empire style of France. But things were changing, especially after the great fires that devastated Chicago and Boston in the 1870s. Architects were beginning to use new structural techniques to build the first skyscrapers, and firms such as Adler and Sullivan, for whom the young Wright worked, were trying to build in a more distinctively American style.

Wright developed these ideas further to make his buildings quintessentially American. Inspired by the open spaces of the Prairies, he developed horizontal, ground-hugging houses with innovative layouts to create buildings that seemed more at home in North America than their predecessors. He used natural materials, too, such as stone and wood, to superb effect, to ensure that his houses were grounded in the American landscape from which they seemed to emerge.

Organic architecture
So this new American architecture was also what Wright called an 'organic architecture'. By this, Wright meant that it embodied a range of ideals – sensitivity to the site, use of natural materials, integration of house and garden, use of the four traditional 'elements' of earth, air, fire and water – that became cornerstones of the kind of natural, environmentally conscious architecture that is now so fashionable. Wright was among the first to express these 'organic' ideals. He also developed ideas such as earth-sheltered building (creating earth banks to protect and insulate buildings) and making full use of solar heat gain through well-positioned windows – and these ideas too are now common among architects who are trying to build energy-efficient, environmentally sensitive structures.

But what makes Wright's buildings distinctive is the combination of this organic ideal with the fact that they are by Wright himself, a designer of vision whose ideas shine through in his greatest buildings. This combination of factors – organic respect for site and the architect's individual vision – can mean that there is a contradiction in his buildings; but this is often a creative contradiction that adds to their interest. For example, the architect's houses are famously horizontal in emphasis, clinging to ground and site; but sometimes a vertical element, like the tower at Wingspread, contradicts this. Such elements seem to go against the principles of organic architecture but lend the buildings a dynamism, a power, that makes them more interesting both to look at and to live in. To create radical principles takes vision; to break them successfully takes genius.

INDEX